T0316748

CAMBRIDGE LIBRARY COLLECTION

Books of enduring scholarly value

History

The books reissued in this series include accounts of historical events and movements by eye-witnesses and contemporaries, as well as landmark studies that assembled significant source materials or developed new historiographical methods. The series includes work in social, political and military history on a wide range of periods and regions, giving modern scholars ready access to influential publications of the past.

State Aid and State Interference

George Baden-Powell, KCMG (1847–98), graduated from Balliol College, Oxford, before studying at the Inner Temple in London. After a varied career as a commissioner in Victoria in Australia, the West Indies, Malta and Canada, he became the MP for Liverpool Kirkdale in 1885. He also found time to observe the total solar eclipse of 1896 in the Arctic, and co-write a paper about it for the Royal Society. He was a passionate advocate of free trade within the British Empire, and wrote extensively to support the cause. First published in 1882, this classic work on economics sets out Baden-Powell's case for imperial free trade. In the first chapter he sets out his arguments; the rest of the book is devoted to presenting his evidence and comparing the relative merits of protectionist and free trade economies around the world.

Cambridge University Press has long been a pioneer in the reissuing of out-of-print titles from its own backlist, producing digital reprints of books that are still sought after by scholars and students but could not be reprinted economically using traditional technology. The Cambridge Library Collection extends this activity to a wider range of books which are still of importance to researchers and professionals, either for the source material they contain, or as landmarks in the history of their academic discipline.

Drawing from the world-renowned collections in the Cambridge University Library, and guided by the advice of experts in each subject area, Cambridge University Press is using state-of-the-art scanning machines in its own Printing House to capture the content of each book selected for inclusion. The files are processed to give a consistently clear, crisp image, and the books finished to the high quality standard for which the Press is recognised around the world. The latest print-on-demand technology ensures that the books will remain available indefinitely, and that orders for single or multiple copies can quickly be supplied.

The Cambridge Library Collection will bring back to life books of enduring scholarly value (including out-of-copyright works originally issued by other publishers) across a wide range of disciplines in the humanities and social sciences and in science and technology.

State Aid and State Interference

*Illustrated by Results in Commerce
and Industry*

GEORGE BADEN-POWELL

CAMBRIDGE UNIVERSITY PRESS

Cambridge, New York, Melbourne, Madrid, Cape Town,
Singapore, São Paolo, Delhi, Tokyo, Mexico City

Published in the United States of America by Cambridge University Press, New York

www.cambridge.org
Information on this title: www.cambridge.org/9781108036849

© in this compilation Cambridge University Press 2011

This edition first published 1882
This digitally printed version 2011

ISBN 978-1-108-03684-9 Paperback

STATE AID

AND

STATE INTERFERENCE.

STATE AID

AND

STATE INTERFERENCE.

*ILLUSTRATED BY RESULTS IN COMMERCE
AND INDUSTRY.*

BY

GEORGE BADEN-POWELL, M.A., F.R.A.S., F.S.S.

LONDON:

CHAPMAN AND HALL, Limited,

HENRIETTA STREET, W.C.

1882.

Lond* :
R. Clay, Sons, and Taylor,
Bread Street Hill, E.C.

PREFACE.

THERE come upon nations epochs when, rising superior to all experience, a blind dash is made in some unlooked-for direction. This is an infatuation of the national brain which destroys, in the brief period of its rage, the hard-won results of centuries of toil and progress.

A nation comes into being and grows with surprising rapidity till it attains to great stature : it puts on and uses the strength of a Samson But, in those days it not unfrequently happens that the nation suddenly sets itself to sap all the foundations of its greatness : to permit the cutting off of the seven locks of its mightiness. And the Delilah of its destruction is Government Interference.

Has England, in these latter days, fallen under the glamour of such an influence ? Government Interference can only enter where private judgment has

been beguiled to place itself in the embrace of
Authority. And in England, in recent years,
Authority in Matters of Politics has striven, and
striven with some effect, to supplant in the affections
of the people that far more wholesome and beneficial
faith which rested upon the teachings of Political
Economy because these were based upon the sure
and certain warranty of experience.

But if Rationalism in Politics is thus flat heresy
in the eyes of this Authority, is it so in the eyes
of the great intelligent portion of the nation? The
answer is to be found in the fast-growing public
appreciation of statistical information, and the widespread study of this science legislators are called
upon to ignore.

One of the most important of the problems dealt
with by Political Economy is the question of the
effect of State action. And it is by the analysis of
achieved results that we can best tell whether, as a
matter of fact, the State assists most or injures most;
whether its action is best described by the term Aid
or the term Interference.

The State, by direct action, influences the working
of land and labour and education, and other matters
of the first moment to Ireland and to Scotland and
to England, as well as to all the world. But in this

volume I limit myself to results that have been recorded of State action in regard to industries and to commerce.

In the first chapter I summarise the general conclusions to which the details of the succeeding chapters lead.

Some of these detailed results I had already published in the *Nineteenth Century* for July, 1881, and *Fraser's Magazine* for the same month; and in the *Fortnightly Review* and the *Westminster Review.* The Editors of these various reviews have very kindly granted me permission to republish these articles in this book, and I take this opportunity of recording my thanks for such permission.

G. B. P.

8, *St. George's Place, London.*

CONTENTS.

CHAPTER I.

CHAPTER II.

b

CHAPTER III.

CHAPTER IV.

CHAPTER V.

CHAPTER VI.

CHAPTER VII.

CHAPTER VIII.

CHAPTER IX.

STATE AID

AND

STATE INTERFERENCE.

CHAPTER I.

STATE AID AND STATE INTERFERENCE.

§ 1. Political Economy and Ignorance. § 2. The Duty of the State. § 3. Protection in the United States. § 4. Bounties. § 5. High Tariffs for Young Communities. § 6. Free Trade for the British Empire. § 7. Freedom for British Agriculture. § 8. Freedom for British Manufactures. § 9. State Interference with the Commerce and Industries of other States.

§ 1. In these latter days signs are not wanting of the reappearance of an influence that has before now destroyed civilizations. It may be that in England the people are endowed with strength sufficient to combat and throw off this influence; but the struggle bids fair to be severe, even if there be no doubt as to the final result.

B

Authority, in these latter days, is attempting, with daily increase of force, to usurp the sovereignty of liberty.   And in England the evidence of this is seen in the growing tendency to set up individual men or individual ideas in the seats of power that should be occupied by the cultivated national opinion, or by personal knowledge of facts.   In England at the present moment the principles and creeds of sections of the community, that claim to be not the least advanced, degenerate in reality on the one hand into an unquestioning acceptance and worship of mere words, and on the other into an equally unquestioning and unthinking servitude to men who are blindly supposed to embody some idea.

There is evidence that an appreciable portion of the educated intellect of the nation may fall into this bondage of hero worship.   If the result be of sufficient power to enable a Government to ride roughshod over all principles and experiences that would otherwise check some particular political move, there is at once risk of an undoing of all that has been done; of a loosening of the whole national fabric.   The turning into the road to ruin is made immediately Government undertakes to do what is, and has been, best left to private initiative.

Popery in politics is the resource of nations or

of individuals, of low intellectual calibre. Unquestioning surrender of the political conscience to
some human high priest, is the refuge of the
incapable and the ignorant. Authority, in the matter
of politics, only becomes personal with those who
lack power or energy to think for themselves.
Authority may be well defined as "the allowing
some one else to think for you." And in this sense
it would appear, in these latter days, Division of
Labour has been carried to a pernicious extreme.
For instance, if Political Economy is banished by
Authority to Saturn, many there are, and these
passing for intellectual men, who have been found
to bring their lips to say, "So much the worse for
political economy."

There is but one silver lining to this cloud of
dependence on others. The cloud itself is some
check on that yet more baneful tendency of the
times—the tendency of educated ignorance to
assert itself. Argument, snatched hurriedly from
the skurry of modern life, is mistaken for fact;
second-hand and often interested explanations are
mistaken for the occurrences they would explain;
and this half-knowledge, which is altogether worse
than no knowledge, is only too ready to pose before
the world as knowledge, and to usurp the place of

teacher that of right belongs to experience. In
reality, all this misleading mass of assumptions
and vain theorisings is after all only formulated
ignorance. It is thus possible even to welcome
Authority in politics if only it prove to be some
antidote to this other great political evil. But this
welcome is altogether soured when we find the
High Priest of this Authority himself suddenly
discarding knowledge and experience, ridiculing the
teachings of history, and telling us that the science
which collects and explains all that is known of
the results of human action, is no longer of any
service in mundane affairs. Such ideas can only
flourish where there prevails actual ignorance of
the true nature of the science of political economy.

The abstract principles of Political Economy are
nothing more nor less than logical explanations of
successful human work. The science is thus an
exact science in so far as it collates the recorded
results of such work. It can describe by analysis
and abstraction each of the conditions which when
co-existent make up necessarily a certain effect.
It can tell us, with all the certainty of mathematics,
that certain defined conditions existing together
are a certain total or effect, for this effect is merely
a bundle of conditions.

Ask Political Economy, "what is the cause of manufacturing prosperity?" It will reply : Take any case of manufacturing prosperity and you will find you have a community enjoying, as much as, or more than, its possible rivals, a favourable climate, skill in the people, energy in the people, an adequate command of capital, an adequate command of raw material, and liberty to utilise all these conditions. Free Trade does not cause it: Protection does not cause it: for it is nothing more nor less than the realised co-existence of several conditions, each one of which can be seen by analysis to exist in all cases of manufacturing prosperity.

Political Economy unties for inspection the bundle of conditions that, in its entirety, *is* some definite effect or fact. It describes each of these conditions, and it explains once and for all that if you take these several conditions and make them up together into a bundle you will have such and such a particular effect. It is a necessary truth. It is this analysis of results which is the main function of the Political Economist. His chief duty is to explain economic experience. His " principles " are the constants he finds in circumstances; the substantial conditions which underlie circumstantial varieties. He does not explain on hypothesis; he simply draws up a list of the actual conditions which must be present together if we are to have any given effect.

§ 2. So far as private acts go Political Economy has less to say than in the case of public acts; and there is no more important problem to be explained by Political Economy than the question how far the common body politic—the State—is to do the thinking for the community, and interpose in the regulation of private acts.

If we look to history we find that all prosperity is generated in freedom. Anything and everything that interferes with freedom generates a negation of prosperity. And the State, the expression of the unity of any community of men, has the one whole duty of securing the freedom of the individuals who make up the community. But it is a community; and the true freedom of the individual is liberty for the full play of his own energies limited by the precisely similar liberty for every one of his fellow-citizens. The guardianship of these liberties is the prime function of Government—the one great final cause of its existence. The State has to hold the true and just balance between the individual and collective liberties; and in the economic quite as much as in the moral or religious affairs of mankind, the State can do harm by letting alone, but it also can do harm by not letting alone. In other words, there can be State Aid as well as State Interference.

It might be said that it is the duty of Government to bring all previous experience of the human race to bear directly upon the particular conditions in which a nation may find itself, and so forestall much lengthy trial and consequent waste of energy. But it is often the case that Government itself is in error, and is more liable to act on wrong judgment than the private individual. And this is specially the case in industry and commerce, because these thrive best under the impulses, sacrifices, and knowledge of the individual. Before now, States, in their endeavour to promote some industry, have choked out of it all its life; States have succeeded in setting up unprofitable industries; States, in their endeavour to hasten industrial development, have been known to foster industries by no means profitable to the community at the sacrifice of those that were in reality the most profitable. All this is never possible if such development be left to individual initiative. The individual best discovers what is profitable and what not: the individual best bears the losses incident to failure. It is of the first importance that every individual be left free, and neither encouraged to take up unprofitable nor hampered in the prosecution of profitable industries. It is folly to encourage a man to make hats when he might be more profitably employed growing wheat. It is folly to check his making hats when it no longer pays him to grow wheat.

It is held to be an open question whether in actual life a man's acts are governed by reason as often as they are directed by unreason. This latter—this unreason—is the arch enemy of progress—the subtle destroyer of systems of civilization. And as reason is founded on experience, so is unreason founded on ignoring experience. And this experience is a knowledge of the several conditions that make up the bundle that is known as the effect. Unreason is the negation of experience, and thrives only under the supremacy of ignorance.

Luckily at the present day ignorance has acquired the habit of formulating itself with as much exactness as knowledge; and we can cull from the popular arguments of the day the definite contentions advanced by this formulated ignorance, and compare them with actual fact.

In analysing results it is right to go into detail; to separate the sticks of each bundle; to enter at length into the description of the many conditions we find combined into each result. And I summarise in this chapter the analysis of the bundles or effects which are analysed in detail in the succeeding chapters.

In Industry and Commerce there is one great lever to State Interference, known to the world as "Protection." It is the interference by Government with what is imported into a country for the avowed purpose of securing certain ends for the home industries and commerce. It is thus that investigations naturally group themselves round the problem—Is Protection, in the popular sense of the term, State Interference or State Aid? Does it assist or impede wholesome natural development?

§ 3. Among the formulas that have become the stock-in-trade of this Ignorance none is more frequently met with than the pointing to *the United States as an example contradictory of all that is credited to Free Trade.* We are told, How is it, if all this be true about Free Trade, that the United States, with their stringent Protection, develop so fast, manufacture so much, and are generally so prosperous? The sum total of the answer is that in every point in which the United States do flourish and prosper it is in spite of, and not because of Protection. The chief sources of wealth over the vast interior—the foods and the raw materials—are being worked under the stimulating ægis of absolute Free Trade. By the constitution of the United States it is strictly forbidden for any one of the States to levy customs duties on goods entering from any other State.

And the United States are as large as Europe and as rich in all natural wealth. The high tariff can affect this community in two ways. In the first place it affects alone by imports ; and the population of the United States imports but 2*l.* per head as compared with the 10*l.* per head imported in the United Kingdom. In the second place, the high tariff is supposed to yield revenue, and so relieve the nation of other taxes. But if we look to records, we see that within the last ten years the customs revenue, from yielding 19*s.* per head of population, has fallen to yield only 11*s.* and that the actual bulk of the annual yield has decreased 25 per cent. Thus the high tariff fails to relieve the country of other taxation; and at the same time it presses comparatively lightly on a population that buys so little abroad.

The question remains, What of the positive effects ? Protection was instituted to develop

manufactures, and yet the percentage of manufactures to the rest of the commodities exported is
not only insignificant in amount, but dwindling
year by year. Imported manufactures still hold
their own in the American market; and all that
can be said in the summing up is that Protection
has fostered the growth in America of manufactures
that are a dead loss to the community at large,
and has stifled some industries that would have
been of the highest national advantage.

§ 4. Formulated ignorance sometimes shifts its
ground. "It may be true, all this about Free
Trade and Protection; but Bounties, at all events,
must be fought by direct action." To understand
this problem aright it is well to have before us
the whole details of some typical case; and there
is no case more distinct, more recent, and more
fully recorded than that of the Sugar Bounties.
If we look into such details we at once find that
Bounties in the result do more actual harm to
the nations that give them than to the rivals they
attempt to overthrow. A Bounty is a portion of
the national wealth handed over by the State to
an individual. It is a tax on the nation in favour
of some individual. It is presented to the individual for carrying through some industry. If that

industry be profitable in itself the Bounty is an entirely gratuitous gift. If that industry be unprofitable in itself the Bounty is merely a bonus on pursuing an industry which decreases the national wealth. A Bounty is thus a tax on the people, which is at best an altogether unnecessary drain on their resources, and which may be, and in many cases is, a direct encouragement of a waste of the nation's resources. A Bounty is indeed a political sop that many a dishonest Government has thrown with great "politician" effect. But in the end it brings ruin and loss. It either encourages an industry that needs no encouraging, or it encourages an industry that should never be encouraged.

In regard to Sugar Bounties we find that those countries which give no Bounties possess the most flourishing sugar industries. It is usually found that where one industry or country receives a Bounty other industries and other countries clamour for them. The movement, like other Protective measures, tends more and more towards a drain on the popular wealth for the sake of a few individuals. It is distinctly against the general prosperity, and subversive of the conditions best for the particular industry itself. If the Shipping Bounty in France, for instance, proves a "success," it will be a new burden of taxation on the French people equivalent to an additional 4*d.* in an Income Tax. So long as the French are willing to support this burden, so long do they handicap themselves in every industry to this extent against English competition. The same is the case with Sugar Bounties. We are told an Import duty of 2*s.* a cwt. on all sugar we import that has received any Bounty would countervail the effect of the Bounty. In other words, if the English taxpayer will kindly contribute a sum of 600,000*l.* the effect of the Bounties will be effectually neutralised. Because other nations handicap themselves in their sugar industries we are asked to do so likewise. By their Bounties some nations send us refined sugar at a price lower than they could otherwise afford to sell at ; and other nations send us raw sugar at a similarly reduced price. Continental taxpayers, in short, pay to the continental refiners and growers part of the price the English ought to pay for their sugar. This is the sum and effect of their Bounty giving. And we find on the continent a widespread and general outcry against these Bounties, chiefly based on the fact that England, the only country that has cut herself aloof from all such restrictions on industry, is the only country in which the sugar industries flourish and increase.

§ 5. Formulated ignorance is fond of asserting that *Protection, though altogether wrong for fully-grown communities, may yet be beneficial for young communities.* Luckily recent history has provided us with a test case. Two of our own colonies, of sufficiently similar size and environments, have been racing together for ten years on the rival systems of Free Trade and Protection. The value of this test case has been fully acknowledged. Indeed the comparison of Victoria and New South Wales has recently become a commonplace with political economists. At the meeting of the British Association, in 1880, I first put forward some statistics of the ten years' progress of these two colonies. These figures I have since elaborated, and they have been extensively quoted. I set them out afresh in this book, as they prove conclusively that in all desirable growths, in the details of revenue raising and the promotion of manufactures, as well as in the general advance in prosperity, a low tariff does far more for a young community than a high tariff.

Formulated ignorance is also fond of asserting that a country that keeps its own tariff low while other nations retain high tariffs is adopting a policy of *one-sided Free Trade* that must in brief space prove its ruin. In answer to this popular fallacy it is well to remember there are in this world Free-ports— communities that actually levy no customs duties whatever. If we look to Hong Kong, for instance, we find an island in close contiguity to a highly " Protected " populous and industrious continent. In Hong Kong there are no import duties whatever; and yet here we have a, community advancing fast in prosperity ; raising an abundant revenue ; and attracting a fast-growing population increasingly em- ployed in the arts of civilization. Those who object to a low tariff on the incomprehensible plea of " one-sided Free Trade " will do well to ponder over this instance of a country flourishing with no tariff at all.

§ 6. Formulated ignorance has, in these latter years, become much enamoured of the idea of *a Zoll- verein for the British Empire.* Free Trade within the Empire to be extended to all foreign countries willing to afford reciprocal advantage, but with a rampart of protective duties against all others—this is the policy suggested. It is admitted that Free Trade is best ; and next, the definition of Free Trade is abandoned, and restrictions on commerce ad- vocated. *Free Trade is the doing away with all that practically interferes with the free course of industry*

and commerce. We are told this is impossible over
the whole world at the present—but it is possible
over the wide British Empire. Next, the assumption
is made that all the Colonies are willing, provided only
we hedge the Empire round about with a wall of
protection. And we are told the whole of this grand
effect is to be produced by the imposition of customs
duties on certain commodities so long as they come
from foreign countries unwilling to concede reciprocal
trade advantages.

That Free Trade is possible over the wide British
Empire is perfectly true. Indeed, over the whole
Empire there are only two fiscal authorities out of
forty that are not at this moment pursuing the wise
policy of Free Trade. The advocates of a Fair Trade
Empire will find themselves grievously mistaken if
they rely on the illusion that the Colonies are
willing to join a Free Trade Bond, provided only it
be surrounded with a wall of higher duties to outsiders. The Colonies understand their position too
well. They trade largely with every nation under
the sun. It is true they buy most of their manufactures in England, but they send great proportions
of their own produce to foreign nations, and by
selling abroad they are enabled to buy in the
mother country. All the Colonies wish for tariffs

everywhere as low as possible. With true practical insight they will be found very averse to the provoking a general raising of tariffs. It must also be remembered that the imposition of customs duties in England on certain goods, if of foreign and not colonial origin, would be of no real effect. If such a measure were to have its apparent effect, it would enable the Colonies to send to England, for instance, all their wheat, and with the profits they would purchase the wheat they required for their own consumption from foreign nations. The same amount of wheat would be grown in the same places, but this interference with the free course of commerce would force it into different markets.

The true foundation for a Free Trade Empire is the national conviction that low tariffs are most conducive to prosperity. This conviction is already widely held by the free congenital communities of the British Empire. The cases of Hong Kong and of Victoria and New South Wales are evidences that this conviction is sound and good. That the conviction should increase in strength, and spread till it inspires the whole nation is dependent on the problem whether Englishmen all the world over will shape their policies by the light of experience, or grope, as other nations have done to their ruin, in

C

the darkness of fictions and fancies that are
pleasurable at the instant, but have no foundation
in fact.

§ 7. Formulated ignorance is particularly strong
in its assertion that the policy of *one-sided Free
Trade has at all events ruined the Industry of Agriculture in England.* We are told that now when
lean years come the farmer gains no compensation in
rise in price for shortness in quantity. It may be true
that if we still levied a duty on foreign wheat, in
lean years prices would rise somewhat more than
they do in the absence of any duty.

But the extent of their rising would be small. Our
present surroundings force us and enable us to
import more than half of the wheat we consume;
and the cost of production of these importations
would have a corresponding effect on prices in
England, duty or no duty. The enormous advance
in facilities of transport has had far more effect on
the wheat supply than any mere alteration of import
duties in any one country. If duties kept prices of
wheat high, it is perfectly obvious no duty-imposing
country would care to sell its wheat in the low-
priced English market. Supposing, however, a duty
is placed on imported wheat, the question remains,
would the farmer be better off? Beyond all doubt

he now-a-days obtains the "raw materials" of his industry at far less cost. Oil-cake of every kind, Indian corn, and other foods; manures; implements, both as to variety and quality; all these he obtains better and cheaper, because the supply is free from all State Interference. Of his land it cannot as yet be said that it is free from State Interference; but even in this respect the Free Trade of his country has enabled him to acquire sufficient use of the soil at very low cost. Wealth, acquired in so many other ways than agriculture, seeks satisfaction in an ownership of the soil, which has no ulterior object in making use of the soil. Consequently it becomes true that if we look to all the agricultural requirements—to proximity to good markets, to fertility of soil, to climate, to supply of labour, and so forth, we find that it is in England the farmer pays least for the use of good agricultural soil. This is due to the general prosperity. And the farmer feels the effect not only in regard to land, but also in regard to labour. A very fragmentary rise in the prices of food and lodging and clothing would tell disastrously for the farmer in the price of labour. So far, then, as the "raw materials" of his industry are concerned, the absence of State Interference is an unmitigated blessing for the farmer.

There is the further important element of the
prices he can obtain for what he produces. We
hear frequently of the very low price of wheat. It
has been low lately, but it has been lower in previous
years, and there is compensation in the fact that
barley and oats are higher. The average prices per
quarter of wheat, barley, and oats for five year periods
during the last forty years have been as follows :—

	1841-45.	1846-50.	1851-55.	1856-60.	1861-65.	1866-70.	1871-75.	1876-80.
	s.	*s.*	*s.*	*s.*	*s.*	*s.*	*s.*	*s.*
Wheat ...	54·9	51·11	56·4	53·4	47·6	54·7	54·7	47·6
Barley ...	31·0	31·11	31·2	38·9	32·11	38·11	38·10	36·5
Oats ...	20·7	21·4	22·10	24·5	21·10	24·6	26·3	24·3
Average for all grain crops	35·5	35·1	36·9	38·10	34·1	39·4	39·11	36·1

Wheat follows the general modern tendency
towards lower prices in all things, but its price also
exhibits a tendency to greater steadiness, the more
its exchange is free. During the past forty years,
for the four decades, the range of wheat prices was
for the first decade, 25s. 6d. ; for the second, 36s. 2d. ;
for the third, 24s. 3d. ; and for the last only 14s. 10d.
Moreover, there is little doubt but that the very low
cost of prairie grown wheat will soon be a thing of
the past. Rapid increase of population on the prairie
itself has run up the value of the land. This at

once makes it necessary to farm, and not merely to crop. Moreover, fifty millions of people will soon come to live on these prairies, and they will consume a large proportion of the wheat there produced. With the exception of this prairie cropping, wheat is produced in England as cheaply as anywhere; and, with the prairie cropping at an end, there will be no further fall in prices, but every certainty of a moderate rise over the whole world.

And all this while, with continued fall in the prices of his own " raw materials," the farmer has seen a continued rise in the price of meat. This will not be checked; for in all new lands meat will never be lower in price than it now is.

So far as the great industry of Agriculture in England is concerned, its permanent success has proved that it flourishes, because instead of State Interference, it commands that State Aid which sets about abolishing any impediments to the free course of the industry. Here, indeed, there is grand scope for reform in England. Several recent laws have incidentally become unfair burdens on Agriculture; many old laws have survived the time of their useful existence, and also grown to be burdens on Agriculture. In both cases reform is urgently necessary; and in both cases Agriculture may look for very con-

siderable relief and assistance if the State will only
aid to abolish both new and old State Interference.
And the country will have to look for such reform to
some new party, for the agricultural legislation
recently initiated by one great party in the State is
marked not only by the banishing to Saturn of the
teachings of experience, but also by fundamental
ignorance of actual agricultural life. And as a
consequence, however good in intention, it fails to
achieve any practical end that is good.

§ 8. We are told Agriculture is the greatest of
English industries, and we have seen that State
Interference is its bane. We are told we are a
nation of shopkeepers, and no one doubts but
that a policy of Free Trade promotes commerce
and exchange. We are told we are the work-
shop of the world. But here formulated ignorance steps in and tells us that the absence of State
Aid for our manufactures is rapidly ruining the
country in its capacity for manufacturing. We meet
with a variety of formulas. We are told *"foreign
countries shut us out with increasingly hostile tariffs."*
We are told our Colonies do the same. And yet if
we look round we find that, as a matter of fact, on
the continent of Europe there has been for many
years a growing tendency to lower tariffs, to reduce

the number of items in tariffs, and to grant to us most favoured nation treatment. If we compare continental tariffs of 1880 with those of 1860 we find that in fourteen out of the sixteen countries they have been lowered. In 1860 the average number of items on these tariffs was 140; in 1880 it had fallen to 112. In 1860 seven out of the sixteen countries granted us most favoured nation treatment; in 1880 fourteen granted us the favour, and the remaining two had expressed their willingness so to do.

And when we turn to our Colonies we find that only two out of forty maintain tariffs that can in any way be described as high or hostile. One of these instances is that of Canada, and here the high tariff was made to include English goods, not out of hostility to English manufactures, but because the Supreme Government of the Empire maintains the theory that no duties within the Empire are to be differential. Moreover, as a matter of fact, both these high tariff Colonies continue to import more and more of our manufactures. For instance, even in effect, there is no hostility to British manufactures in the records of Canadian trade: English imports are increasing and United States imports decreasing steadily.

We are also told *foreign countries are flooding us
with their manufactures.* But foreign countries are
not increasing their export of manufactures so fast as
England increases hers. If foreign countries· are
flooding England, England is flooding them in far
greater proportion. It is also remarkable to notice
that foreign countries increase their exports both in
quantity and kind in proportion as their tariffs are
low in the particular items exported. Nor is this
contrary to reason. A protective or high tariff is
only effective against goods that can be produced
cheaper elsewhere. Consequently these goods will
drive from all other markets similar goods made in
the protected country.

If foreigners were supplanting us as manufacturers,
not only in our own markets but in foreign markets,
we should at once see the effect in our imports and
our exports. Now, as a matter of fact, the percentage of manufactured articles to the rest of our
imports is insignificant—only eight per cent., and it
does not increase. And, on the other hand, as a
matter of fact the percentage of our manufactures to
the rest of our exports is very great—ninety-four per
cent., and does not decrease.

Other countries range through the whole gamut of
State Aid from the negative pole of Free Trade to

the most positive pole of Protection. But England continues steadily at the head of the list of manufacturing peoples. Her supremacy seems to be assured. And this for the chief reason that the State sees the folly of attempts at Aid which are in reality nothing but hurtful Interference. Wisely in England the State confines itself to securing to every worker as a consumer the advantage of obtaining everything he uses or consumes at lowest possible cost, and as a producer the security that to whatever industry or task he may devote his energies he may rest practically assured that his energies are not being misapplied, for they are applied under the searching influence of open competition with all the world. In such a free atmosphere the risk of misapplication of energy is reduced to a minimum; and, at the same time, advantage is taken of every facility of production the wide world offers.

§ 9. But in these latter days the State has been asked to aid and *to interfere, not only within its own frontiers, but within the boundaries of foreign states.* England has been asked by a section of her citizens to force foreign nations to lower their tariffs; to force foreign nations to abolish the Bounty system; and to bind foreign nations to admit English goods

on certain terms by the aid of commercial treaties.
The means that we are told are the only available
means mark the unwisdom of any such policy. We
declare that low tariffs are good and high tariffs bad ;
and then, in order to prevail on other nations to
lower their tariffs, we are to threaten to raise our
own. We declare Bounties to be bad; and then, in
order to prevail on other nations to give up the
system, we are to threaten we will injure ourselves
to the exact amount that these Bounties injure the
nations that give them. We declare there should
be free exchange of commodities between all nations ;
and then, in order to obtain this free exchange, we
are to propose to bind ourselves to some particular
nation by a treaty arrangement of "reciprocal
advantages" specifically curtailing our freedom of
exchange with third nations. These means are, on
their very face, inconsistent with the attainment of
the end desired. They are means that have invariably
commended themselves to governments for many
years. They are means that have invariably failed.
They are means that must be once for all discarded.

The various States of the world are politically independent of one another. Any agreements between
them must be in the nature of free contracts. But
these contracts have this fundamental distinction from

contracts between individuals, in that there is no superior compelling power to enforce their fulfilment. War or necessity are the sole ultimate arbiters. Conference, arbitration, and agreement may be appealed to, but subject only to voluntary concession. To injure ourselves in order that others may not injure us is a course of policy neither wise nor useful. And yet such a principle is the basis of all these policies by which we are to interfere directly to reform other nations in regard to commerce and industry. It is ultimately a waging of war. We know it will cost us much; we say we must go to war, for there are no other means of compelling nations to do what we wish them to do. If, however, we turn more thought into our consideration of the case, we discover that this kind of warfare has never been successful; that it not only fails to attain its end, but that it necessarily costs more than any gains it can win.

And all the while we forget that to keep the peace will induce the very results we vainly seek to bring about by war. We wish for freedom for commerce and industry. We wish to see this freedom prevailing in every State. We wish to see no one state, by its individual action, curtailing this freedom in all other states. We, and other nations,

have tried war for many years. We have endea-
voured to secure this freedom for all by denying it
to ourselves. Other nations, all the world over,
have done the same. More recently England has
turned back from these illogical courses. England
has said, " So far as in me lies I will commence by
giving myself this freedom. If it is this great good
we all conceive it to be, results will soon prove that
I am right." And results are conclusively proving
the wisdom of the new English policy. Other European nations are now beginning to ask how it is
that England and Belgium and Holland and Switzerland are drawing right ahead of all others as
commercial and industrial nations. The Australian
colonies are asking why is it that New Zealand
and New South Wales are outrunning Victoria.
The United States are asking why is it that unprotected England floods American markets with
her manufactures, and also drives American goods
out of neutral markets. The high-tariffed States
of South America are asking, " Why is it we have
to go to free-trading England for our manufactures
no less than for our capital ? " These results must
tell, and are telling. It is the force of successful
example which will lead other states to set themselves up free in commerce and industry. It is to

this teaching we must trust for a coming emancipation of nations from State Interference. The means
to this end is the spread of knowledge. Ignorance
is the arch enemy to the spread of commercial
freedom. Cynics may ask whether the printing
press has in the sum total done more to disseminate
and give authority to ignorance than to knowledge;
whether it has established in the public mind more
untruths than truths. At all events, the printing
press may be made the vehicle of facts. And it is
to the wide, universal publishing of recorded facts
we must look for restoring to experience a measure
of its lost influence in public affairs. A public
opinion ignorant of and despising experience is the
canker that eats the heart out of a nation and
thereby brings about the ruin of its civilisation.

And experience tells us that in order to secure
the highest and most lasting prosperity for commerce and industry, *State Aid should be invoked
or utilised for the sole purpose of disestablishing
State Interference.*

CHAPTER II.

THE FAILURE OF PROTECTION IN THE UNITED STATES.

§ 1. The case of the United States important. § 2. The Causes of their Prosperity. § 3. American Manufactures. § 4. Revenue from Customs Duties § 5. Protection in each case hostile to advance—Its Future.

§ 1. THERE are Free-traders and Free-traders. Some men are Free-traders because they know Free Trade to be best; more men are so because they think it to be best; most men are so because they believe in their chosen teachers. These two latter classes are, indeed, imbued to the backbone with the idea that Free Trade means wealth and prosperity; but at certain seasons they become the unwilling victims of most awkward questionings both from within and without. Members of Parliament have been found to ask such questions; and, in the *Times,* a " Letter from Mr. J. Bright on Protection" figures with strange frequency. These letters are almost invariably in answer to the evident, if cleverly concealed question, "If Free Trade be all you say, how is it that the United States flourish so under a *régime* of Protection?" This question implies either a sad lack of detailed knowledge on the part of the interrogator, or a criminal expectation of such a failing on the part of his victim. It is my present purpose to put forward the plain matter-of-fact rejoinder to this specious question.

Such an investigation has a present and particular value in that incidentally it elucidates problems of the first importance to our own farmers and landowners, no less than to our manufacturers and exporters. The supply of the English market with wheat and meat; the supply of the United States market (a vast market, embracing such items as the construction and maintenance of the one hundred thousand miles of rails that will soon be "in work" in the States); the existence and growth of manufactories of various kinds on the other side of the Atlantic—these and others are all problems closely connected with this investigation, and problems of the first moment to all thinking Englishmen. . . . .

§ 2. These inquiries range themselves under several heads : (i.) How far is the prosperity of the United States connected with the prevailing policy of Protection ?   (ii.) How far has Protection succeeded in setting up native manufactures ? (iii.) How far has Protection succeeded in supplying funds to the revenue ?   (iv.) How about this Protection in the future ?

How far is the Prosperity of the United States connected with the Policy of Protection ?—This first question lands us at once among the circumstances that combine to bring prosperity to the United States; and if we look in vain among these for the influence of Protection, it may surprise the thoughtless into attention to facts, but it will in no wise run counter to the convictions of those who know.

Protection may be defined as the interference by a Government with the influx of commodities produced in other States in order to serve certain ends in regard to its own industries.   It is obvious, then, that Protection affects a country by the means of its imports; and in judging of the causes of prosperity in different States, Protection will avail as a factor in proportion to the comparative importance of the imports.   For instance, the British Isles import annually an equivalent of 11*l.* per head of

population; the United States import annually but
2*l.* per head. Thus, it may be said that in the
United States the direct effect of a policy of Protection on prosperity (for or against) is only one-
fifth what it would be in England.

But this minimised influence of Protection is
further lessened by the fact that the United States
is eminently an underpeopled, undeveloped country.
This fact, it will be seen, is at once the basis of the
national prosperity and the more than sufficient
antidote to the action of Protection.

Evidence of this is seen in the recent high-pressure development of the industry of supplying food
to Europe. For some years past this tillage and
pasturage of the prairie has produced an enormous
surplus of food supplies. These would have been
mere valueless commodities, or rather would not
have been produced at all in such quantities, but
for the fact that cheap means of transit happened to
coexist to convey this surplus to European and other
markets. Thus it became wealth; and was used in
great measure to repay other nations some of the
capital they had advanced to render such things
possible. Of the total annual exports from the
United States nearly one-half consists of this food
surplus. It is thus evident that this production

D

alone of food from virgin soil—supplying as it does the first necessaries of the large home market, and paying for two-thirds of what the nation buys abroad —is accountable for a major portion of the prosperity enjoyed by the United States.

But if to this food surplus we add the exports of "raw-materials"—of cotton, minerals, and so forth —we shall account for at least eighty per cent. of the total annual exports from the United States without trenching in the least on the domain "fostered" by Protection. It is then not difficult to see that the prosperity of the United States depends on industries that have no cause whatever to thank Protection.

These industries, however, are rapidly discovering cause for curses and not thanks. Farmers find the high tariff raise the prices of all agricultural tools and implements; millers complain of the high cost of machinery for mills; carriers of the high prices of the metal-work for elevators and for railways. Experience is proving that duties which protect one class necessarily injure all others. The train of cause and effect runs in the well-known circle. Each manufacturer finds that, though the duties that protect him are said to be ultimately paid by the consumer, nevertheless the consumer has his natural revenge in that everything the manufacturer uses or consumes in the process is enhanced in price.

It is no long task to show that the prosperity of the United States exists in spite of, and not because of, Protection. And this is so even when no mention has been made of the most important fact in connection with this prosperity. Too seldom do we remember that absolute Free Trade has been long and firmly established throughout the United States, and that it exerts an influence many many times greater than that exerted by Protection. Free Trade reigns absolute and supreme within the frontiers of the United States. This is a fact writers and speakers on both sides the Atlantic are too apt to overlook. The full import of this fact is seen when we remember that the rapidly increasing population, already numbering fifty millions, only imports from abroad one quarter of the value of goods that the thirty-three millions of the British Isles import. *And the vast and important home market of so very large and so very self-dependent a population is regulated entirely on principles of absolute Free Trade.*

The importance of this fact is all the more evident if we remember that the United States is about as large as Europe, but with only one-seventh

of the population. We have indeed a territory
equalling Europe in extent and in variety of soil,
climate, and product. But properly to picture the
case we must sweep out of Europe all the English,
Dutch, Danes, Swedes, Germans, Russians, Austrians,
Italians, Swiss, Spaniards, Portuguese, and Turks,
and then distribute and settle over the whole area
of Europe the population of France and Belgium
only. The British Isles would proportionally receive
about the population of London to work up their
prolific resources, their mines, their pastures, their
fertile soils, their ores, their fisheries, and so forth.
Then, if we add to such distribution of population
perfect freedom of interchange of products all over
this Europe, we have a picture of the condition of
the United States at the present day. It has been
the dream of Cobden's disciples to extend Free
Trade over Europe. *Our American cousins have long
ago and definitively established Free Trade over an
area equalling that of Europe.*

It will be immediately evident that the prosperity
that ensues in the United States will be due to this
freedom of exchange and this comparative paucity
of people engaged in the highly profitable task of
developing vast virgin resources. Of a truth, so far
as its prosperity is concerned, the United States is

a glaring instance of the high economic value of
Free Trade. In the United States we have a group
of communities, large and small, young and old,
under-peopled and fully-peopled, and with every
variety of human and natural forces, all bound one
to another in the fertilising bonds of Free Trade.

Such is the prosperity of the United States; such
the foundations of this prosperity. Protection, in-
fluencing only by means of a comparatively insignificant import trade, is but a weakly drag on this
prosperity, which thus rests in reality, both in
regard to home consumption and to export, on
Adam Smith's "plenty and cheapness of good land,"
coupled with perfect freedom of exchange over the
length and breadth of this good land. Protection
in the United States occupies an altogether subordinate position as a direct factor for or against this
prosperity; and there is force enough at the present,
in the development of the splendid virgin resources
of this partially-peopled Free Trade continent, to
induce prosperity in spite of, but not in consequence
of, Protection.

§ 3. *How far has Protection succeeded in developing
Native Manufactures ?*—In disposing of this second
question we are faced at the very threshold by the
fact that the genesis of manufactures in the United

States occurred under exceptionally favourable auspices. Gold and other populating magnets had attracted across the Atlantic swarms of emigrants from Europe. A very large percentage of these were skilled mechanics and manufacturing hands, and these were, frequently, the men of highest spirit and energy in their various callings. Thus the States had simply to utilise, and not to create or even to introduce, the best skill, traditions, and experience of the old-world manufactures. And there soon came about a general willingness on the part of these immigrants to revert to their old callings as opportunity offered ; for the new toils of unwonted agriculture, or the disheartening failures on multitudinous dummy gold-fields, gave fresh prominence to memories of former more lucrative and more satisfactory work. Manufactures were engrained in the people before arrival. These habits and traditions of work needed only time for their reappearance ; but it was sought to hasten this reappearance by the curious self-sacrifice of all other interests in favour of these manufacturers.

And yet, if we look to the surroundings of the manufactories of the United States, we see at once that their very life is closely bound up with the existence of undeveloped virgin resources. When bad times come and consumptive demand wanes, then short time or stoppage of mills, and so forth, merely throws more human energy into the opening up of unbroken agricultural areas. A great increase in agricultural output is the result, and, provided a market be found for this, a recuperative force is at once set in motion which shrouds the fact that many of these artificially supported mills and factories are not in unison with the true life of the community. And, in addition, the ready supply of food offered by virgin soil does away with any risk of actual starvation.

In spite of these manifest "natural" advantages, we nevertheless cannot be blind to the notorious fact that in bad times there is more actual distress in the manufacturing districts of the States than in those of crowded but Free-trade England. The special reason of this is that bad times prevent production at profits ; and that although man can cease being a producer for a time, he can only cease being a consumer by leaving this world. And it is on man as a consumer that Protection presses with so heavy a hand. So far as Protection has any effect in America, it enhances the price of everything to the consumer, and this forces the manufacturer, capitalist, and workman alike to suffer more than need be when bad times force him to stand by in idleness as a producer.

And again, in prosperous times American manu-facturers enjoy very considerable advantages—not because of Protection, but because of this wealth of virgin resources. A great store of provisions and of raw material is readily amassed ; and the demand of prosperous times readily converts this into wealth. The workers on this raw material reinforce willingly that class of consumers who are lavish and extrava-gant in their expenditure. This style of improvident consumption has, as a matter of fact, become a marked feature in the United States whenever eras of prosperity set in ; and it is a style which is always above paying heed to the fact that prices are so greatly enhanced by the incubus of any par-ticular commercial policy. Home consumption becomes thus specially brisk, even to the extent of causing a decrease in exports. And so an important but artificial and unwholesome stimulus is given to the protected industries which completely shrouds the evil results, to the consumer, of pro-tective duties. This unnatural vitality is the certain precursor of a crash such as that which fell upon the American people in 1873. This wealth of virgin resources at once nourishes and conceals that diseased condition of the body of manufacture which is induced by Protection.

It is well also to consider the influence of this protection of manufacture in the United States on the supply of the home and the foreign markets. In the first place, in the United States it has been estimated that only one-tenth of the whole population are even connected with manufactures. Such a percentage, if we regard the records of other communities, may fairly be set down as the unaided issue of mere concentration of population : it certainly shows that Protection has failed in any appreciable manner to divert human exertion from its natural channels. The attractions of an underpeopled soil are too great to allow of the population being *forced* to other labour.

Evidence of this is found in the failure of the American manufacturers to supply their own home market even with wares for which they enjoy special facilities. This result is greatly aided by the fact that high prices of American made goods consequent on the high tariff act as an antidote to that tariff so far as foreigners are concerned. English cutlery, for instance, in normally prosperous times successfully competes with American even in the Western States. Of Sheffield cutlery the States imported

74,000*l.* worth in 1880, as compared with 50,000*l.*
in 1879.   The revival of trade last year immediately
doubled the importation of iron and steel from
England.   It is a curious sight to see *free* Americans
submitting to the fact that English iron and steel,
burdened with cost of transit and a 40 per cent.
duty, can yet undersell American steel in the
American market.   When the railway system of
the States is completed there will be about 100,000
miles of rails laid.   The mere maintenance and
necessary renewals over these lines implies an
enormous and persistent demand for rails.   English
makers continue to hold their own in this division of
the American market, and it is satisfactory to
remember that the low price at which their Free-
trade opportunities enable them to supply these
rails adds to the wealth-producing and purchasing
power of our friends the consumers of the United
States.

Increase of population creates new markets, which
the population naturally endeavours of itself to supply.
And wherever population congregates in sufficient
numbers, there the necessary industries arise—*if
they can.*   In America the manufacture of iron and
steel has struggled into existence, but as yet it has
only so far succeeded as to compete as it were on

sufferance with the supplies sent all the way from England. Protection keeps the prices of labour and of living so high, that the "prohibitive" duty on English supplies, instead of keeping them out of the market, simply becomes a bounty paid by the inhabitants to enable the English manufactuer to penetrate into the market. Meanwhile no one knows whether the free manufacture of iron and steel can be carried on in the States cheaper than the importation of foreign iron and steel. If it can, the Americans are buying their iron and steel now at a dead loss to themselves. If it cannot, they are paying to their manufacturers the annual losses on a process of manufacture that does not pay. *That they lose by the transaction is evident ; the only question is as to the greater or lesser amount of their loss.*

Thus Protection resolutely prevents the Americans from obtaining the command of their own home market even in those wares for which the country *may* possess special aptitudes ; and at the same time it prevents the Americans from finding out which manufactures pay, and which do not. The great fact remains that the high prices consequent on Protection do actually act as a powerful antidote to the high tariff, and pay for foreign manufactures the

entrance fees into the American market which
Protection extorts.

In regard to the supplying foreign markets, it is
but logical to suppose that if Protection have its
claimed success in starting within a community industries specially suitable to the circumstances of
the community, there will be some surplus products
of these industries for export. How do the manufacturers of the United States fare in foreign and
neutral markets? That they penetrate to them is
not to be gainsaid. But that they penetrate in
insignificant quantities is seen from the fact that
only one-tenth at the most of the exports of the
United States are articles manufactured in the
States. And even this export trade is manifestly
a mere result of the peculiar conditions surrounding
manufacture in the States. Americans have developed an extraordinary ingenuity of invention;
they have also developed a tendency to "do things
big." If the opportunity is favourable they thus
manufacture large stocks of articles whose novelty
and neatness is often their chief recommendation.
But for the present the export of many such articles,
often the mere realisation of some gigantic scheme
of advertisement, or the getting rid of articles
for which there is absolutely no sale in the home

market, is because of depression in the States. It is clearly recorded that American drills and sheetings only appear in the great China market when periods of severe depression exist in American manufacturing centres. The cost of production in normally prosperous times is too high to favour export. The stocks that even then accumulate become unsaleable when good times return; these are added to the stock manufactured under the cheapening pressure of depression; and the whole " lot " is eventually to be got rid of at abnormally low prices.

As a general result it has been noticed that just now in the United States with prosperous years the imports increase and the exports decrease; whereas the contrary seems to be the case in years of depression. Protection increases cost of living; it raises prices all round; wages come to be normally at abnormal heights. In prosperous years the local manufacturers having to pay higher wages can only sell at excessive prices. Americans are asked to pay these prices; and they do so in prosperous times. But these same high prices, instead of fostering local industries, simply enable the less costly foreign commodity to enter the market even though saddled with the extravagant duty Protection imposes. The result is that imports increase and the local manu

facturers cease exporting. But they also cease
selling, even in the home market.

However, with times of depression these things
alter. Americans no longer buy. Prices are too
high. In their own phrase, they "scrape through"
till times mend. Imports decrease. Local manufacturers have stock in hand they are unable to
get rid of in the home market; they also find
labour willing to put up with lower wages, and
it comes to be possible to export that for which
there is no sale whatever at home. Exports increase.
American manufacturers once more appear in foreign
markets.

It is necessary to remember, in this connection,
that in England, if industrial energy cannot find
vent in the creation of a margin at least of exportable wealth, industrial pauperism must result.
In the United States, on the contrary, this
energy is not so confined; it can and does seek
profit from the appropriation and development
of virgin resources. Labour and capital find
their natural field in the prairie and not in the
factory. It is only in abnormal times of severe
depression that these natural conditions are tem-
porarily suspended and industrial energy creates
any margin for export. Manufacturing enterprise

thus harassed will never achieve any palpable place in foreign markets till the United States become fully peopled up. It would seem only natural that, for the present, the export trade of this large population should be almost all made up of the crude products of the soil—cotton, minerals (solid and liquid), and food—all endeavours of Protection to the contrary notwithstanding.

This tendency is amply verified by records. The United States Government publish what they term a "percentage of agricultural products (including products of the forest) to total of domestic products exported every year." It is well, in order to eliminate temporary influences, to take the average annual percentage for four-year periods. For the past sixteen years these averages have been 68, 74, ·76 and ·79 per cent. Records show there has been a steady rise of this percentage all the while that stringent Protection has been endeavouring to decrease this percentage. These are facts, not fancies.

On the whole, then, Protection in the United States, so far from encouraging and fostering the growth of manufactures, seems, if we look to results, only to hamper and harass those to which concentration of population has given legitimate

birth; and at the same time to shield others which
have but doubtful claims to legitimacy. It shields
them from a justified death only with the assistance
of forced contributions levied as black mail from
a heedless and unthinking people. There may not
be consciousness of this in those who work these
industries; but, they are the chiefs in the ranks
that oppose Free Trade; and their impelling motive
is the sacred motive of self-preservation.

§ 4. *The Revenue Argument.* — Protection in
America finds much political support in the plea
that money must be raised for carrying on the
government of the country. General Hancock's cele-
brated "Tariff letter," during the late Presidential
election, summarises this question in the words—

"The necessity of raising money for the admin-
istration of the government will continue so long
as human nature lasts. All parties agree that the
best way for us to raise revenue is largely by the
tariff. So far as we are concerned, therefore, all
talk about Free Trade is folly."

It is, at the least, remarkable to find such
language uttered by a prospective head of the
Democratic party; but the sentence is a fair sample
of the plea put forward, even by the genuine
Protectionist, in favour of high tariffs. Americans,

as a matter of fact, have exhibited marked distrust of direct taxation. To escape that method they seem to be content to make large sacrifices. They are told with truth that much revenue may be raised by customs duties. But to argue thence to the conclusion that therefore "all talk about Free Trade is folly," is to miss the point of the argument. The interested manufacturers contrive with ease to fan this plea into the flame of stringent Protection to their own special manufactures. With ease they lead their fellow-countrymen—who in the vast majority have little direct connection with external commerce—to the conclusion that if revenue is to come of customs duties, the higher the duties the greater the revenue.

This revenue argument has been urged by Prince Bismarck in Germany, as well as by Americans, and it is above all the one plea on which this retrograde policy has now and then commended itself to the practical British Colonist. "Theoretical" economists, indeed, point out that to tax your trade is to destroy your trade; that "where Protection begins there revenue ends;" that to hamper the entry of goods into your market by heavy duties is to starve the goose that is to lay the golden eggs of revenue. More practical economists will hold that

E

it is a mere question of balances; and that it is conceivable that the duties may be so cunningly adjusted, that while inevitably destroying some of the trade incident to the smaller duties, they yet suck more actual revenue out of what remains.

The question is really solved only by appeal to experience. The United States, with all the acknowledged evils of a high tariff, extract a revenue of 27,000,000*l*. out of the trade of a population of fifty millions. The United Kingdom, enjoying the manifold benefits of a low tariff, extracts a revenue of 20,000,000*l*. out of the trade of a population of thirty-five millions. In either case the populations contribute revenue through the customs to the annual amount per head of eleven shillings. But the English population enjoys in addition all the pecuniary benefit of a trade three times that of the Americans.

Besides this, if we compare the customs revenues of England and the United States for even the last ten years, we see that the English receipts maintain a steady level of 20,000,000*l*. per annum, while those of the United States have *fallen steadily* from 37,000,000*l*. in 1869 to 27,000,000*l*. in 1879. During this period the English population increased by four millions; but no less than ten millions

more human beings have come to live in the United
States. In other words, by looking to these records
of what has been, we find that with a low tariff a
population contributes far more revenue through the
means of customs duties than with a high tariff.
The high customs duties in the United States have
failed altogether to provide that steady uniform
contribution to the revenue that the low English
duties have provided. They have in ten years
rendered this particular source of revenue 25 per
cent. less profitable, though population has increased
30 per cent.

This result is no doubt partly due to the fact
that high duties inevitably give birth to manifold
methods of evasion. It would be an interesting
calculation to discover how much the signal decrease
in American customs' receipts is due to this cause.
Smuggling only finds sufficient inducement under
high tariffs. And smuggling is nowadays of extensive variety, ranging from the simple landing
of a cask of spirits while the eyes of the revenue
are turned the other way, to the elaborate machinery
of dishonest middlemen who thrive by false pack-
ing and false " declarations." By this means silk
has been known to " pass " in casks " declared " as
bottled beer. And the extreme is reached in the

E 2

brazen-faced bribery which is so well known in
sundry of the more backward European ports, even
though we refuse to credit the tales of travellers
as to its existence in some of the landing places of
the most advanced community of this age of progress.   These widespread systems of fraud can only
exist in the atmosphere of high duties; but in that
they flourish to artistic perfection.   We hear, for
instance, of men who will buy steel rails in Europe,
" lay " them, run an engine and two trucks over
them, take them up again, and pass them through
any " amenable " custom-house as " old ' or " scrap
iron," thereby reducing the duty by three-fourths.
These things may be possible under the paramount
influence of railway " rings "; or they may be facili-
tated by cases (however singular and rare) of guilty
connivance in the custom house.   The importers
do not, probably, pocket the whole of the duty
evaded ; some of it, no doubt, disappears elsewhere;
it is a tax on their trade, but it is a tax which
fails to swell the revenue.

Altogether it is found by the actual experience
of both methods that the contention of raising
revenue is altogether in favour of low tariffs. High
tariffs destroy the trade, and breed methods of
evasion.   These methods reap no profits under low

tariffs, while trade by low tariffs increases fast. This question of revenue is settled no sooner than an appeal is made to experience; but hitherto in the United States the great majority have confided in the interested minority, and have failed to satisfy themselves that high tariffs in any way contribute to the revenue in proportion to the asserted ratio.

§ 5. *The Future of this Protection.*—In conclusion, it remains briefly to consider the future of Protection in the United States. We are met on the threshold of this inquiry by the pertinent question, How is it that, in the face of the proverbial "Yankee 'cuteness," such a state of affairs should be permitted in the United States ? It is, in truth, not a little astounding that Protection should be for one moment tolerated in States whose original and grand historical claim to independence was liberation from bondage to the mercantile theory. It is a strange contradiction to have to recognise the high intelligence of the citizens of the United States, and in the same breath to detail the follies and evils of the commercial policy which they have adopted in their dealings with foreigners. It is a strange contradiction (and one that has been published in the States) to find the shrewd American

citizen allowing himself to be governed by men
who said some years ago, " You must not trade
with Texas—it is not national territory ; " and who
this year say, " No impediment whatever shall be
allowed in the way of your trading with Texas;
it is now national territory."

The primary explanation of this paradox is that
all evidences of evil are, as it were, gilded over by
the flood of wealth that overflows from the opening
up of new resources. It is true the high tariff
simply lessens, *pro ratâ*, the savings or profits which
naturally accrue from the employment of capital
and labour. But in a new country (and a country
whose soil yields annually some 10,000,000*l.* of
gold, besides abundance of other minerals and
endless agricultural products) these profits accumulate with a rapidity altogether unknown in
fully developed lands: and the incidental loss
passes unheeded.

Again, in a land of unbounded virgin resources,
food, or the possibility of its acquisition, is ready to
the hand of every man. In such a land a number
of even useless manufacturers are supported without complaint, for the stomachs of the people do
not feel the sacrifice. And it is an old tale that
when the more animal portions of the human

body are in comfortable circumstance, the head is inclined to deal indulgently by objectionable concerns with which it has no palpable or immediate connection.

These conditions account in great measure for the fact that a large nation, ever clamorous for the post of guardian of human freedom, should voluntarily place itself in the bondage of Protection. Each free American citizen at the present moment is in the toils of a villeinage to his superior lord, the fostered manufacturer; week by week he hands over to him, under the guise of increased prices, so much of the earnings of his labour, or of the profits of his capital. But he heeds not his position, because his opportunities bless him with abnormally good earnings and high profits.

The conditions under which Protection exists in the United States may be grouped in four categories:— (1) plenty and cheapness of virgin resources; (2) the inflow of foreign capital; (3) ultimate government by manhood suffrage; (4) vested interests fostered by Protection. How long will these conditions remain in effective co-existence?

(1) The first of these groups will for years to come divert the major portion of the national energies to work that has little or no direct connection with

the foreign import trade. The farmers and miners of the west and north, and the growers of cotton and breeders of cattle in the west and south, will, for years to come, have little personal feeling in the matter of a policy directly affecting only the manufacturers of the east. But as population increases—and the process gives every sign of high-pressure speed — these now outlying districts will become central; and to their inhabitants will become obvious and palpable the burden of a high tariff. Indeed the farmers of the west are already complaining of the high cost of the implements necessary to their peculiar system of husbandry. And as population increases, the inevitable increase in output of commodities will demand not only an outlet, but some equivalent return trade. Already western farmers are prognosticating a day when England will be purchasing her wheat where she can pay for it with her manufactures. This result will ensue whenever a rise in the cost of American wheat raises it to the same price in the English market as Continental or Eastern wheat.

The Census of the United States, taken on June 1, 1880, tells a significant tale. During the last decade there has been added to the population 10,000,000 souls. One quarter of this increase is due to immigration, and three quarters to national growth. In the north-east, in the older, *more fully peopled and manufacturing States,* there has been the least increase, amounting only to 15 per cent. In the south-east, among the older agricultural districts, the increase is greater. But in the whole of the wilder west, *where manufactories are conspicuous by their absence,* there the populations have doubled in many instances, trebled in Kansas, and actually quadrupled in Nebraska and Colorado. Mining and agriculture may be said to have absorbed eight out of the new ten millions of inhabitants. This forebodes a coming alteration in the balance of the forces that naturally regulate external commercial policy.

(2) This rapid development of virgin resources is assisted in its tendency to upset high tariffs by the gradual cessation in the inflow of foreign capital and the concomitant growth of the investment of American capital abroad. This change in the tide of capital has already set in. Protection has of late years largely prevented repayment in kind. The foreigner wishing to trade has had to finance :—funds, securities, shares, have passed to American ownership. It will thus come to pass, that if Americans wish to export (and this wish will be largely stimulated as their country becomes opened up) they will be

forced to import by way of repayment. This will be
possible only with a less prohibitive tariff.

(3) These tendencies towards Free Trade will have
a severe struggle with the two last of our four
groups. It has been said that wise men learn from
the experiences of others, but that fools can only
learn from their own. At the present time ultimate
political power in the States is largely in the hands
of those who ignore knowledge of ascertained human
experiences; and who at the same time fail to
win the guidance of those possessed, aud disinter-
estedly possessed, of such knowledge. These masses,
it would seem, must in a measure await the teaching
of their own experience — though the spread of
education will hasten their due recognition of the
experiences of others. But their present prospects
of good guiding are far from hopeful. Facts tell us
that they become the ready instruments in the hands
of those who trade upon their ignorance and upon
the essential human tendency to lend willing ear to
all that flatters innate selfishness. Thus, to win the
votes of wage-earners in America no more powerful
political cry has been devised than that of " pre-
serving Americans from the competition of the
underpaid labour of Europe."

It appears for the present hopeless to point out

that, as a matter of fact, Protection does *not* accomplish this end. The wage-earner in the manufacturing districts is by no means so well off as he would be in the manufacturing districts in England. It has over and over again been pointed out how well the American politician knows the electioneering value of appealing to the nominal rates of wages, but carefully omitting all reference to relative purchasing powers. The American wage-earner may be sure of one point: whatever work Protection brings him, whatever work he gets and would not get if competition were free, has to be paid for by him out of the wages he gets for doing it. Five cents per yard on cotton prints is the duty charged to countervail English facilities of production. The American manufacturer thus charges four cents more per yard for the cotton prints he makes. This protection enables him to make cotton prints and employ people in the factory. But the wage-earners so employed have to pay four cents more for every yard of cotton they buy. And, not only so, but, while they get wages from one industry only, Protection influences many others as well, and all prices are enhanced above what they otherwise would be. *This extra charge on all he buys is the direct effect of the competition of the "underpaid" labour of Europe.*

Protection is powerless to prevent the effect. All
Protection does is to shift the charge from the producer to the consumer; and the wage-earner, if
a producer in the factory, is all the more a consumer at home. Manhood suffrage in the less
settled districts is not yet sufficiently bound up
with the foreign trade to care to busy itself
with foreign policy; manhood suffrage in the
more settled districts awaits the spread of knowledge to force on it a due appreciation of its real
position.

(4) For the present, the most serious and distinct
obstacle is the powerful one of vested interests. The
manufacturers, chiefly located in the eastern States,
derive most benefit and relief from protective duties.
These duties are paid by the nation at large, and a
major portion of the contributions come from other
distant districts. These manufacturers thus thrive
on the contributions they levy of their heedless distant countrymen. Protection institutes rates for
the support of two classes of persons—the one class
consisting of those who could live, and live better,
without this aid : the other class consisting of
those who, without this aid, would have to turn to
other modes of livelihood which would be a gain,
and not a loss, to the nation at large. Industries

involving legitimate national superiorities would flourish all the better without Protection. But industries of the illegitimate kind, whose works are so much waste of energy, inasmuch as they make goods that can be made cheaper elsewhere at the present; industries which will come into being unaided when times are ripe for them—these would perish in the absence of Protection. Such manufacturers owe their all to Protection; of this they are well aware, and they accordingly put forth every nerve to keep their hold on a system, in the absence of which they must devote their energies to other work. The vested interests, of a type altogether pernicious to the general well-being, thus exert their influence in exact proportion to the harm they do to the State as a whole.

Their power was exhibited in the late Presidential election; the Democratic candidate was forced to woo their favour by a partial recantation of the wise doctrine adopted by the Democratic party, that the tariff should be arranged with a view to revenue only. The sop of "incidental Protection" was thrown, though without effect. These particular vested interests know they stand or fall with full-bodied Protection, and their present power is well exemplified in this violent political endeavour to win their favour by the surrender of an important principle.

This necessarily cursory view of the facts of the case brings us, then, to four conclusions :—

(i.) The prosperity of the United States is due to plenty of fertile virgin soil, to great mineral and natural resources, and, above all, to the strict freedom of trade over the whole United States continent. The protective tariff simply impedes this prosperity.

(ii.) In regard to the setting up of manufactures, the high tariff succeeds in hampering those to which concentration of population gives legitimate birth : and in upholding those which are, at all events for the present, a dead loss to the community at large.

(iii.) American (and other) politicians maintain that the high tariff is a good method of raising revenue ; but facts show us that even within the last ten years this high tariff (in a variety of ways) has cut down by nearly one-third the actual amount of revenue formerly derived from customs duties, and which, in a more healthy condition of things, must have in some measure kept pace with an increase of population during the same period of more than one-third.

(iv.) The intelligent American citizen puts up with

Protection because it affects him but little in his absorbing occupation of opening up the vast interior. The assured success of this internal development, coupled with the ebb of foreign capital, will gradually overcome both the heedless *vis inertiæ* of manhood suffrage and the knowing *vis motiva* of vested interests.

CHAPTER III.

BOUNTIES.

§ 1. Bounties never likely to succeed.   § 2. Attempts to revive Shipping Trade in the United States.   § 3. Similar attempts in France.

§ 1. IN Bounties, above all other schemes and policies, State interference assumes most cunningly and most successfully the trappings and outside semblance of State aid. Under the guise of assistance to the native and discouragement to the foreign producer of a given article, many a Government has won popularity for itself from an ignorant and thoughtless people by the simple device of instituting a Bounty system. And the more their ignorance of their own trades, the more their innocence of their own true interests, the more these fostered classes admire and support a Government which promises to protect them by Bounties against foreign competition.

Happily in England most of us feel strongly that Bounty-giving is nothing more nor less than taking money from the great body of taxpayers and handing it over to a few privileged individuals, in order that these latter may carry on industries that might not otherwise pay. Even supposing that Bounties give artificial advantage to any special industry, yet this artificial advantage all comes out of the pockets of the people at large. Bounties may for a time give an artificial and temporary stimulus to a trade, but such stimulus seems invariably to suck the life out of the community, and to leave the field eventually in possession of those foreign rivals who have preferred the wholesome food of free enterprise and the bracing air of open competition.

Bounties are pleasing to the sense of self-interest, to the selfishness of the class in whose favour they are imposed. But this means, that if once you allow or adopt the principle of Bounty-giving, the granting a Bounty to one trade or industry simply provokes other trades and industries to claim similar treatment. The State which grants Bounties to sugar-refiners soon finds itself compelled in very fairness to grant Bounties to shipbuilders. And the future looms dark with the forms of all other

F

industries, possible and impossible, hovering round to claim their share in the generous distribution of the public moneys.

And for similar reasons such a policy adopted by one State provokes other States to similar action. States are very apt to follow one another's blind leadings. Sugar Bounties have been instituted now in several European countries, simply by reason of the strange idea that if Bounties are given to foreigners Bounties must be given to natives as a protection. And when this plea of "fairness" once steps in, nothing more is heard of the fact that Bounties do more harm than good to the trade and to the country which the Government seeks by their agency to aid. People forget that Bounties come eventually out of the pockets of the taxpayers; and they forget what is of yet more direct importance, that Bounties have never yet succeeded in winning a victory against those communities which refuse to have anything to do with their suspicious aid. In this and the following chapter I wish briefly to collect certain recorded results of two illustrative classes of Bounties—those given to promote shipping and sugar industries respectively.

§ 2. It is probable that in few States have more stringent measures been taken to foster a shipping

trade than in the United States. It is certain
that in no States has there ever been a greater
collapse of the shipping trade than in the United
States. The facts of this collapse are the "commonplaces" of all literature dealing with such subjects.

Here again there crops in and acts as a chief
element the necessary evil of all such State interference. With shipping, as with sugar and all
other industries, there are two distinct industrial
phases or divisions; and they are, in their very
nature, antagonistic to one another if once they
are to be "fostered" out of any common funds.
These two phases are those of production and of
use. If you protect the production of ships, in so
far you limit their use; and if you protect the
use of ships, in so far you limit their production.
In the United States it was sought to encourage
shipbuilding in the country by prohibiting the
importation of ships and by encouraging the native
building of ships. Immediately the shipowners found
they were hampered in the supply of ships. Ships
cost American more than they cost English owners.
American ships were no longer purchased, and
then, as a consequence, they were no longer built.
At the same time the shipbuilders had been protected, and so could not object that other industries

should be protected likewise. And shipbuilders found, to their cost, that they had to pay for their material and for their labour far more than shipbuilders in other countries that had no protection· And now all the American seaboard is crying out for the remission of all duties on the materials employed in shipbuilding, and for the removal of all the burdens that Protection imposes on the industry.

Meanwhile American shipowning has died down, and shrunk to comparatively nothing from its former dimensions. The Great War no doubt had considerable effect, but that effect should be past and gone before now; and the Americans must often sit down and look at the flags flying thick in New York harbour, and ask themselves how it is that they are nearly all those of a nation which makes every endeavour to free all its industries of all State trammels, of all so-called State support. No doubt England has unrivalled capacity for production in her readily available stores of coal and iron, but America also yields large quantities of coal and iron, and her woods are at least as good and as plentiful as those of the British Isles. Her seaboard is long, her harbours numerous, and her population much given to maritime pursuits; and yet her shipping industries cannot do more than struggle to maintain a precarious existence, clogged and handicapped by vigorous State support, and altogether unable to compete against the free and altogether private enterprise of the shipping industries of the United Kingdom.

§ 3. With this clear example before her we find France, already with a very respectable marine, nevertheless deliberately devising a new scheme of bounty protection to her shipping trades. As with all such State interference so with this; so great is the number of technical and legal formalities, that the effective operation of the law is seriously impaired. However, after overcoming these, the French Government offers definite money Bounties to those who build vessels in France or to those Frenchmen who own seagoing vessels. The Bounties are not given to Lines otherwise subsidised by Government. They are given on tonnage built in France and on the number of miles run at sea by French-owned vessels. It is at once evident there is considerable contradiction involved. France pays nearly 1,000,000*l.* per annum in subsidies to steamers for carrying mails. By this new law a steamer, provided she does not carry mails, becomes entitled to a subsidy or Bounty. And then again a Bounty is given for

making long and numerous voyages. This bounty
is 1f. 50c. per ton per 1,000 miles. For a trip across
the Atlantic and back a French-built steamer of
3,000 tons receives 1,000*l.*, provided she carry no
mails. If she be English-built she receives 500*l.* It
becomes a question of relative cost of English-built
and French-built ships. If the Bounty on building fail
to make good this difference, then the French ship-
owner may profit most by using English-built ships.

But suppose that this act succeeds to the full in
its purpose. Suppose it doubles the French mercantile marine by adding one million tons of French-
built shipping, and sends this million tons voyaging
over the seas, at average voyaging pace. Suppose this
continues for five years. Then the French taxpayers
will have to provide say 15,000,000*l.*, or, in other
words, pay to French shipbuilders and shipowners
3,000,000*l.* per annum for doing nothing but mind
their own business. And this payment includes
measures for defeating its own end, because it
includes the enabling French owners to purchase
foreign-built ships even when these are dearer than
French-built ships. As we have seen in the Atlantic
trade, an owner may run an English-built steamer
for a year against French-built mail steamers on
equal terms, because he will obtain a Bounty which

they will not obtain. If this Bounty-law were to
raise French shipping to anything equalling that of
English shipping at the present moment, the French
taxpayer would find himself at least one hundred and
fifty millions sterling out of pocket. The question
remains, would there be any possibility of recouping
this sum out of any trade that could be developed ?
The chances are that the question will never be put
to the test, because there will be severe foreign
competition. France need not fear the kind of
competition threatened by Prince Bismarck—a
competition in kind—a retaliatory imposition of
countervailing Bounties by Germany. But France
will find competition very severe and hopeless with
England. It is not by making the nation as a
whole pay for national shortcomings that any particular industry can be made successfully to compete
with countries enjoying greater natural facilities.
Shipbuilding has grown to be a great industry in
the British Isles, partly because of a natural wealth
in coal and iron ; partly because of a maritime
genius fostered both by geographical position and
by great and world-wide trading propensities ;
partly because of the policy of Free Trade, which
enables the shipbuilder to obtain all the materials he
uses at the lowest possible cost. Other countries cut

themselves off from those of these advantages that
can be acquired, and they are thus the less able duly
to utilise such of those advantages as they may
enjoy by the bounty of nature. If the French or
the United States wish to develop a profitable
mercantile marine, the only road is to reduce and
simplify their tariffs, and then see whether in the
consequent free course of commerce and industry
the shipping trade arise of itself or not. In other
ways they may give artificial fillips, but to the
nation at large the balance will be on the wrong
side; the industry will be fostered at the expense of
the community; money will be transferred from the
pockets of the people to those of a few individuals;
French shipowners may buy more of English shipbuilders, and English shipbuilders may start yards
in France and gather in a harvest of French
Bounties; but in the long run the French people
will find the millions they may spend disappear into
the pockets of builders and owners, and leave France
with no greater increase in her mercantile marine
than has come of all the strenuous efforts to
increase that of the United States.

CHAPTER IV.

SUGAR BOUNTIES.

§ 1. Cane-growing in the Colonies continually advancing. § 2. Beet-growing not due to Bounties. § 3. Neither Beet-growing nor Refining flourish in Bounty-giving countries. § 4. How to do away with Bounties. § 5. British Sugar Industries more prosperous than any others.

§ 1. THE most remarkable case in regard to Bounties is that of the Sugar Bounties. It is a case which has all the advantages of having been well ventilated. Its details have in every respect been worked out and tabulated: and its value and importance are best attested by the virulence of the controversy to which it has given rise. There are few results recorded in economic history that yield such distinct and clear lessons.

It may be well to quote these results as I sum-

marized them in a recent article in the *Westminster
Review* :—

" Mr. Ritchie's Committee was appointed ' to inquire into the effects upon the Home and Colonial
Sugar Industries of this country by the system of
taxations, drawbacks, and bounties on the exportation
of sugar now in force in various foreign countries.'
It is our present purpose to deal specially with the
second of these two provinces of inquiry.

But there seems to be some strange fatality that
appears to haunt the very term ' Colonies.'   No
sooner is this term used than the affairs treated of fail
of just appreciation, not only here in England, but
even in the Colonies themselves.   The very men who
should know most, are often misled themselves into
statements that are hard to reconcile with the records
upon which they themselves found these statements.
In the records of this particular committee there
occur instances of this ; and instances, moreover,
directly compromising the most important points
involved.   For instance, in his answer to question
3,858, one of our most trusted authorities on West
Indian matters tells us that the ' diminished production (of sugar in the West Indies) commenced in
1872.'   But the figures of sugar exported recorded

in the tables provided by this same authority are as follows:—

SUGAR EXPORTED FROM THE BRITISH WEST INDIES IN TONS.

	1871.	1872.	1873.	1874.	1875.	1876.	1877.
British Guiana	89,000	76,000	84,000	84,000	80,000	102,000	96,000
West India Islands...... }	211,000	173,000	195,000	188,000	237,000	214,000	181,000
TOTALS...	300,000	249,000	279,000	272,000	317,000	316,000	277,000

The 'diminished production that commenced in 1872' did not continue even till the following year.

Again, the same high authority tells us (3,960)—

'I think that in, say, ten years, half the production of the West Indies would be knocked on the head altogether; in fact it has begun already. I do not think I should be outside the mark if I stated that nearly fifty estates are in course of abandonment now (1879). I think about fifty have come under my own knowledge, principally in Jamaica; about six or eight months ago, so far as my recollection goes, twenty-six estates were advertised for sale without any buyer.'

This latter sentence somewhat qualifies the former; but if we turn to the Jamaica Bluebook itself, we find recorded in dry and hard official columns that only *four* estates were abandoned during the year 1879. And it is further to be noticed that these four were of very small size, making altogether only 323 hogsheads of sugar, in an island which exports annually over 30,000 hogsheads. Moreover, there is, in the opposite column, the very significant entry of one 'abandoned' estate brought back into cultivation.

It is indeed high time that more attention was paid to the actual condition and the actual prospects of this sugar growing in the West Indies. We shall here briefly lay out the facts of the case, collating all by the aid of recent personal experience in almost every West Indian island. We shall confine our exposition, in the main, to these islands; they yield us three-quarters of our own colonial supply. Sugar that is grown in the Mauritius and the East Indies, in Natal and in Queensland, finds its chief market in the Eastern Hemisphere. It may be noticed incidentally that the local demand in South Africa and in Australia is increasing rapidly, but it is increasing out of all proportion to the increase of sugar planting in these large colonies. In Australia, at the beginning of this century, there was no market for sugar. Now, in the Australias there has come to exist a rapidly increasing population of nearly 3,000,000, and all great consumers of sugar. Over the vast interior of the 'island continent' sugar is among the most important of the 'rations,' which form part of the pay of shepherds, stockmen, and others; and in the cities, that are appearing with such rapidity, well-to-do communities of Englishmen are vying with the mother country in their large consumption of sugar per head. But these West Indies — these 'tropical farms of the British Isles,' as they have been termed —are the English sugar colonies in most direct connection with the English market, and therefore the group of colonies most typical of our colonial sugar industries, so far as they are influenced by European Bounties.

At the very threshold we must notice that there is one great fact persistent throughout the history of West Indian sugar-planting, and that is the fact of the perpetual plaint that all is going wrong. The 'groans of the planters,' that made so great a stir in 1670, have never ceased since then to burden the atmosphere. This is, indeed, fresh evidence in support of the plausible theory that the secret of Englishmen's success is their native propensity to grumble. West Indian planters, like their fellow-agriculturists in England, are never satisfied; and it is well they are not. They will have it that what they attempt is done better elsewhere, and the consequence is that they do things better than they are done elsewhere. They grumble that the French have tramways in Guadaloupe, and with this grumbling they introduce better trams on their own estates.

The outrageous assertions of the present evil effect of the Bounties do not surpass the frantic anticipations of evil which centred, in days gone by, respectively round the abolition of slave labour, the competition of slave *versus* free-grown sugar, and, more lately, the extinction of the sugar duties in England. Forebodings just as dismal, arrays of figures just as curious, arguments just as little founded on fact, cropped up in these episodes, and with the same urgency and the same need of explanation as in this last. But the sugar-growing industry has managed to survive. It may be it has changed; it may be it is destined to yet further change; but its destruction would seem to be as far off as ever. . . . . .

The English public that abolished slavery and the sugar duties, offered speedy compensation in the greatly increased consumption of sugar in England that followed on each of these high-principled acts. In 1840 the total sugar consumed in England was 4,500,000 cwt., its value was about £10,000,000, and the consumption at the rate of 15 lbs. per head. In 1873 the consumption had risen to 51 lbs. per head. The duties were finally abolished in 1874, and for the year 1879 the total of consumption was at the rate of 65 lbs. per head, representing a total of 20,000,000 cwt., for which no less than £27,000,000 was paid.

We are now face to face with the latest phase of these complaints. We are told that the abolition of these duties injured West India sugar-growing by allowing unbridled play to the baneful effects of Bounties that are given in sundry foreign countries on the export of sugar. Incidentally, however, it will be remarked that these very Bounties themselves only exist in countries where sugar duties continue to be levied; and the abolition of these duties in England set up England herself as a most successful example of a country thriving in an atmosphere where Bounties are impossibilities, and where the market for cane sugar is free of access. That this example has not been without effect we see in the fact that the French and other Bounty-yielding countries, are already exclaiming they can no longer compete with English refiners, or with colonial growers of sugar. Thus this much-complained of abolition of sugar duties has in itself come to be one of the most powerful arguments towards the destruction of these very Bounties that are regarded with such pious and unfeigned horror.

Before considering the Bounties themselves, the real measure of their effect, and the best means to their removal, it is well briefly to examine, by the light of recent local knowledge, the present condition of the industry of sugar growing in our West Indian colonies. We shall at once find that these colonies have, during the present century, passed through three periods—the one, of corruption and collapse culminating in the abolition of slavery in 1838; the second, of mismanagement and uncertainty, lasting up to some ten or twelve years ago, when matters became more settled; the third period that has since set in is of steady progress, and of a far more healthy and hopeful tone generally of enterprise and management. The most significant feature of the middle or transition period was the odd reluctance with which those most concerned came to recognise the dawn of new and more favourable conditions. It has always been common to confine causes to the single influence of slavery and emancipation. And this common error is rarely rectified by the altogether necessary, if forgotten addition of the fact, that prices of sugar have seen as great changes as this labour question. In the world's market, from causes quite extrinsic to the West Indies, the price of sugar has since the period of emancipation fallen from 50*l.* to 20*l.* a ton. It is true, that here again the vast increase in consumption which England's free trade policy has enabled her to enter upon, has in great measure compensated this enormous fall in prices. Prices may have fallen to one-third of what they were, but the Englishman consumes just three times as much as he used to do. This would be very palpable compensation, but for the fact that the West Indian growers do not provide him with the extra supply he now consumes. And this is in great measure the fault of the West Indian grower himself: but it is a fault he is fast remedying. His chief obstacle has, hitherto, been his being trammelled at every step by the traditions and the arrangements created by and for a state of affairs that has passed away. And the dying voice of this old dispensation is the present persistent outcry that Bounties are creating much loss, suffering, and injury to our West Indian sugar-growers.

G

As a matter of fact the West Indian colonies, even under present arrangements, seem capable of producing sugar *cheaper* than it can be produced elsewhere, or from other plants.   Mr. Quintin Hogg pointed out (Ques. 3871) : ' You get in saccharine matter *four times* as much to the acre in Demerara as you would get in France.'   Any one conversant with the West Indies will acknowledge that the actual cost of growing and manufacturing sugar ranges from 9*l.* to 12*l.* per hogshead.   The cost of putting this sugar in the English market ought not to exceed 3*l.* or 4*l.* a hogshead.   European beet-root growers and manufacturers universally declare that a price of 18*l.* a ton is a price that will, if per-manent, destroy their industry altogether.   The limit that will destroy beet-growing will only *curtail profit* in cane-growing as at present carried on in the West Indies.   This fact should suffice to show Bounty-giving countries the prompt necessity of a reform of their ways.   The boasted effect of these Bounties is to lower prices in the great English market ; but this, in the end, is to abolish Bounties, by rendering impossible the industry they were insti-tuted to support.   The ' bounty-fed' refiners already cry out.   M. Léon Say himself complains : ' Ce qui est certain, dans tous les cas, c'est qu'à l'inverse de ce qui existe pour les raffineurs Français, les raffineurs Anglais peuvent obtenir leur matière première à un prix inférieur à ce qui devrait être son prix normal.'

Growers are also discovering their error. In his Report for Mr. Ritchie's Committee on the sugar industry in Germany, our Secretary to the Embassy tells us, 'the average cost of manufacturing raw sugar from beet would be about thirty marks (30s.) a cwt.' And at the present, whatever the actual cost of production on the spot, the governments of these countries allow the general public to subscribe to make good any losses the refiners and growers may become subject to, owing to the low prices forced upon the market. How far, and for how long, a confiding public will thus continue this thankless and baneful charity time only can prove.

It is well worth putting on record the figures supplied to Mr. Ritchie's Committee by Mr. Hogg of the export of sugar from the British West Indies. They exhibit a marked, sustained, and definite increase. They, of course, vary from year to year. There are few crops more variable than the cane crop. It will therefore be well to record the totals for four-year periods, and so eliminate this element

of uncertainty, and better fit the figures for general
perusal

EXPORT OF SUGAR FROM THE BRITISH WEST INDIES.

Years.					Totals per four-year periods, in Tons.
1844—47	...	...	...	...	554,000
1848—51	...	...	...	...	544,000
1852—55	...	...	...	...	608,000
1856—59	...	...	...	...	649,000
1860—63	...	...	...	...	754,000
1864—67	...	...	...	...	797,000
1868—71	...	...	...	...	903,000
1872—75	...	...	...	...	900,000
1876—79	...	...	...	...	975,000

From 1844 to 1865—for twenty-one years—the
actual annual total never reached 200,000. Since
1865—for sixteen years—the annual total has never
been below 200,000, except in the two years 1869
and 1872. It will be observed, also, that in the
period 1872-75 there is a falling off, slight indeed,
but still not an increase. This is worth noticing, in
spite of the more than compensating increase in the
next period, 1876-79; this latter great increase. it
will be remembered, comes immediately after the
abolition of sugar duties when Bounties were said
to be of most effect. That this abnormal decrease
was the effect of seasons alone, we know when we
see that the crops of 1872 and 1873 were very much
below the average (amounting but to 400,000 for the

two years); and there is further proof in the fact
that for those two years the prices of sugar were,
in the words of the Report of the Committee,
'abnormally high.'

It is well to notice parenthetically, that, though
the present condition of the industry of sugar
growing in our West Indian colonies is in a condition which enables it to contemplate without
anxiety the competition of beet-root in the future,
it is in a condition, nevertheless, which is itself
capable of vast improvement. Those concerned with
the West Indian industries themselves give palpable
proof of this in the vast sums annually expended
in machinery, and the introduction of improved
methods of cultivation and manufacture. In Bar-
bados, for instance, sugar land fetches nearly 100*l.*
an acre at this day. These prices would not be
maintained in a despairing community.

It has been remarked that the sight, not uncom-
mon in Jamaica, of a ruined windmill or watermill
is a welcome sight, inasmuch as it tells a tale, not
of relapse, but of advance; a tale of the fertilizing
introduction of steam power and fresh skill and fresh
capital; and, in a similar sense, it is true that of late
years the records of estates abandoned, and of estates
sold for what they would fetch, are signs, not of

demise, but of fresh life. In the days of slavery and of high prices estates were started over large areas; in the course of years most of these became encumbered with jointures and charges. In the days of collapse that ensued, both in regard to the labour question *and* in regard to price, the absentee proprietors of these charges and encumbrances let matters ' drift ' in the hope of better times; they looked to the future to solve both the labour and the price troubles. In most cases these estates were owned in groups, and the very favourably situated paid sufficient profit to cover, for the time, the losses on the badly situated. By degrees that were altogether too slow, estates were one by one put out of cultivation or sold; and it is one great advantage of low prices that they considerably accelerate this salutary process. There were many estates continued in working that had yielded profits when sugar was at 50*l.*, but which had no chance of doing so with sugar at 20*l.* There were many estates that could well yield profits sufficient for one or two incomes, even when prices had so fallen; but such estates only too often remained charged with the supply of the five or six private incomes that had of old easily been yielded by the higher prices. It is, then, a gain to all to find the one class of estate absolutely put out of cultivation, and to find the other sold for what it will fetch; and sold, moreover, to new owners who, no longer burdened with the old charges and jointures, may proceed forthwith to make excellent commercial profit out of the legitimate advantages the West Indies undoubtedly possess over most other countries in this matter of sugar growing.

These high prices also helped to maintain among many planters a proud abstention from attempting to remedy the losses and difficulties that had come of the abolition of slavery. There arose, not unnaturally, a bitter class feeling, brooding over the fact that in order to achieve a national object the individual had been made to suffer; there had been an apparent breach of justice, and the injured class sat down on their estates, and when things went wrong, enjoyed an uncouth and baneful satisfaction in proving to the world that the injury done was material. These ideas are not yet completely eradicated, and they are partly to blame for a slowness, apparent most in Jamaica, among planters to improve their cultivation. Already, however, sufficient has been done to prove at once the actual value of these improvements and spread the knowledge that they are possible. Ploughing, weeding,

manuring, and irrigation, have been proved to
greatly increase the quantity of cane to the acre.
Better breeding better care, and better handling of
the 'working oxen,' have curtailed largely the
expenses of 'hauling' or taking the cane to the
mill. Tramways, and 'wire railways' for ravines,
have been introduced with similar effect. The
'Usine' system will probably pay in certain districts when introduced. The railway extensions, and
new coastwise steamers, will largely relieve many
districts of their heavy expenditure in the matter of
the carriage of the sugar to the port of shipment.
Altogether, there are many prospects of considerably
cheapening the present cost of production.

It will be seen then, that, so far as facts go, the
West Indian sugar industry is in a far better and
far healthier plight than it has ever been before.
This industry has, indeed, suffered from two causes
—natural and 'human.' Adverse seasons in the
one case, and our own widespread commercial depression in the other, have acted most deleteriously
on production and on consumption.

§ 2. These two classes of causes have, however, in
recent investigations, been ignored in favour of one
small species of a third genus—the political. And
yet it is difficult—eminently difficult—to trace any

real effect of any magnitude directly to this particular division. The centre of the argument, at
which we have now arrived, is the fact that certain
foreign countries give Bounties on the export of
sugar. We pass, then, to ascertain the real measure
of this effect, and the best means for the removal of
these Bounties.

The battle waged round these Bounties may be
well likened to some mediæval struggle for a
standard, wherein leading knights find themselves
suddenly the cynosure of all eyes; and when the
real contests and material combats of the rest of
the field are forthwith hushed and suspended, as if
by mutual consent, in order that all eyes may feast
on an intrinsically insignificant incident that has
now become the centre and point of all effort. The
possession of the standard in itself is of little value
—so much wood and linen, or, it may be, silk. So
with these Bounties; all other arguments seem
suspended, and the contest centres itself on a something, which, the more we look into it, the less does
it prove to be of material value or influence. As
with the military standard, so these Bounties are
fought over with such fierce excitement that all
inquiry is for the time ignored as to the intrinsic
value of the Bounty itself. Many men rush to the

attack with the battle-cry, 'Bounties lower prices;' they heed not, neither do they require proof of the measure of this asserted influence, or of the connection of the result with the asserted cause.

The whole influence of these Bounties needs to be set out clearly. Many of those interested in the trade have of late years sought to impress the outside public with the idea that Bounties are the cause of *all* these ills. The instinct of the outside public has, as yet, refused to credit all this; and it is well, in the interests both of those concerned in the trade as well as of the general consuming public, to seek out the grounds on which this instinctive reasoning is based.

The Bounties, in the first place, are supposed greatly to encourage the production of sugar from beet-root. Granting that this be so, it is obvious the cane-grower cannot complain, unless this action lowers prices. From some of the Tables in the Appendix to this Report we can cull most apposite figures, even though we regret that these tables fail to bring results further than the year 1874.

	Years—1864.	1865.	1866.	1867.	1868.	1869.
	s. d.	s. d.	s. d.	s. d.	s. d.	s. d.
Prices of cane sugar ...	28 11 ...	23 8 ...	22 2 ...	22 5 ...	24 1 ...	25 10
Hundreds of thousands of tons grown { of beet sugar }	4	5	6	7	7	8
{ of cane sugar }	14	14	15	14	16	16

Years (*continued*)—1870.		1871.	1872.	1873.	1874.
	s. d.	s. d.	s. d.	s. d.	s. d.
Prices of cane sugar ...	24 1 ...	26 3 ...	26 11 ...	23 2 ...	22 4
Hundreds of { of beet sugar }	9	9	11	11	10
thousands of tons grown { of cane sugar }	16	16	18	18	17

We see there is a sustained increase, year by year, in both crops till 1874, in which year there is a slight falling off in both—largest proportionately in the beet crop. We see also that beet increases far faster than cane; and, in the ten years under review, beet, from monopolizing in the first year about 2-9ths of the supply, comes in the last year to monopolize over 3-9ths. But it will be noticed that *prices show no tendency whatever of being affected by the alterations in the proportions of beet and cane supplies.* Commencing at a high figure, prices fall rapidly; but only to rise again nearly to the same height, and then again to fall.

And this relation of price to this beet *v.* cane argument is further illustrated by a table supplied by Mr. Lubbock. In this Mr. Lubbock gives most interesting data in regard to the effect of the detailed growth of the beet crop on detailed prices of cane sugar, and the results are most significant.

Years:—1865.	1866.	1867.	1868.	1869.	1870.
s. d.	s. d.	s. d.	s. d.	s. d.	s. d.
Prices of cane (Trinidad) 21 6	18 8	20 10	22 5	22 11	19 8
Beet crop ; increase or decrease per cent. over previous year's crop. + 84	+ 22	+ 4	+ 1½	+ 27	+ 11

Years (*continued*):—1871.	1872.	1873.	1874.	1875.
s. d.	s. d.	s. d.	s. d.	s. d.
Prices of cane (Trinidad) 23 4	24 10	20 1	19 7	18 4
Beet crop ; increase or decrease per cent. over previous year's crop. − 7	+ 31	− 3	− 5	+ 20

According to these figures, it would strangely appear, *increase in the price of cane sugar is usually accompanied by increase in the amount of beet produced;* whereas, in two of the only three cases when the crop of beet was less than the previous year, there is a decided fall in price over that of the previous year; and in the remaining case there is a decided rise in price in the following year, though the production of beet showed an increase of no less than 30 per cent. We have seen that the consumption of sugar in the world increased during this same period from 18 to 27; that of these proportions, cane supplied respectively 14 and 17, while beet, supplying 4 in the first instance, came to supply no less than 10 in the latter. Beet has thus monopolized the supply of a great proportion of this increased demand; but the figures have yet to be produced, it seems, which shall prove that this new supply is in direct connection with any definite fall in price. Indeed, in the evidence before Mr. Ritchie's Committee, the West Indian planters over and over again assert their confidence in their ability successfully to cope with beet-root competition, 'provided bounties be done away with,' and the two methods be left to unrestricted competition. *It would seem, then, that beet-growing in itself has little to do with this lowering of prices.* The question remains—do the Bounties affect these prices; and if so, to what extent?

When one's own case is good, it is often well to assume, for the sake of argument, the correctness of the evidence brought forward by one's opponent; and in this present case we may even admit, with the most eager opponent of Bounties, that a duty of 2s. on every sort of sugar imported from Bounty-giving countries would effectually 'countervail' the effects of this Bounty. But we must in that case also make it clear that, as at most only one-third of our sugar supply comes from Bounty-giving countries, the actual effect of the Bounties, so far as growers are concerned, is not 2s., but only 8d. a cwt. Again, we see that if sugar (as was stated in answer to question 6028) at the price of 18s. 6d. was being grown 3s. below its cost price, Bounties

at their best, must be merely partial causes of this
effect, even when we allow them the full influence
attributed to them by their most ardent opponents.
And the advocates of this countervailing duty will
have to devise some remedy to correct this larger
class of influences, double the effect of the Bounties,
which, if true and lasting, must absolutely drive all
sugar out of cultivation."

§ 3. But there are other matters in connection with
this asserted effect of Bounties which merit more
attention than they have received. If we look to
*the condition of the industries in the Bounty-giving
countries themselves*, we find much to countenance
Sir L. Mallet's opinion :—

' Ques. 6344.—I myself greatly doubt whether
the effect of this Bounty is such as to enable the
receivers of the Bounty to sell their produce at a
very much lower rate than they would be able to sell
it without the Bounty.'

One thing is certain, that even the keen desire
to do away with Bounties exhibited by English
refiners and importers, is no whit keener than that
shown by Frenchmen, at all events, who are interested in sugar. And these Frenchmen have reason
for their keenness. Among others, they complain of

the fact that the English refiner can, and the French refiner cannot, avail himself of the Austrian Bounty on raw sugar; indeed, French statesmen have already asserted that the Bounty given to French refiners may be defended as the duty that *countervails* the advantages reaped by the English refiners in obtaining Austrian Bounty-fed raw sugar free of duty.

The French authorities gave valuable evidence before the Committee. M. F. Georges described the position of the industry of growing beet for sugar as ' *extremely critical.*' The fabricants, he declares, 'are almost *at the last gasp,* and if they lower the prices of beet the farmers will *entirely leave off growing beet.*' West Indian planters should notice that, even while the dreaded Bounty system lasts, prices are now so low that a fall, even fractional, will prevent beet-growing altogether. Prices, so far as beet-competition is concerned, are at their lowest ebb. But the cultivation and manufacture of beet is at its highest perfection. Neither of these assertions can be made of sugar-cane growing in the West Indies.

M. F. Georges also gives evidence to the effect that sugar-beet production in France is even diminishing, and certainly not increasing. West

Indian growers should pay attention to question 6074 :—

'Ques.—I understand, to summarize your evidence, you believe that Austrian and other Bounties, if they continue, will greatly damage the French growers of sugar?'

'Ans.—It will *destroy the French manufactures entirely* in a certain number of years; that is to say, that the productions will be reduced to a certain extent every year. I would add that, if the price of beet were to be lowered, the farmers would not be able to grow it any more.'

This means the lapse of 400,000 tons of sugar now grown annually, and whether the French refiners are to continue to refine by importing cane sugar (and probably to abolish import duties on it), or whether France has to buy her sugar elsewhere—either way cane growing would be largely benefited.

This is a most useful example of the complexities and intricacies that come of State interference with production. If we abolish the Austrian Bounties, French refiners and French growers continue as now; if we do not abolish the Austrian

Bounties, English growers and English refiners both prosper over French.

And another French authority, M. Fouquet, gives it as his opinion: ' If all the Powers, Austria, Germany, and Belgium, continue to have Bounties, we shall be in a very short time obliged to *leave off entirely making sugar in France.*'

And M. L. de Mot, on being asked—

'Why should the production fall off so much in France while the home consumption is so large as it is at present,' replied, 'Because of the actual price. We sell under cost price actually; and there is no doubt that, if things are to go on as they are, in two or three years production will diminish. . . . . We expect, if things go on as they are, that, next year at least, probably 40 *factories will be closed.*'

From Belgium, the Secretary of Legation reports :—' Very small advantages indeed must have been derived by Belgian refiners from the surpluses (Bounties) they obtain, judging from the fact that for the last fifteen years *sugar refining has steadily diminished in Belgium.*' It is not surprising to find Belgium, as a Bounty-yielding country, eager to abolish Bounties ; they do her no good, for she imports but little sugar. From the Hague comes

H

the same tale of diminishing exports, in spite of
the Bounty which exporters can secure by means of
the drawback. In Italy there is great dread of
Bounties; and both Government and Legislature
recommend 'that no time should be lost by the
Government in entering into negotiations with other
States interested in the sugar question, with a view
to taking measures for guarding against the con-
version of drawbacks into Bounties.' In Germany,
as the industries, both of sugar growing and of
refining increase, so does the revenue derived from
sugar fall off, because incidentally the exports increase and take so much the more in drawbacks.
And the German refiners themselves make an interesting complaint. They say, concerning 'moist'
sugars :—

'Nor can the German refining industry compete
in these products with English refiners drawing
their supplies of *German raw sugars* from Germany,
inasmuch as Germany pays a larger drawback of
duty on the export of raw sugar than would be
paid proportionally on the export of the refined
sugar produced from it.' And their report proceeds : 'The German refineries buy duty-paid raw
sugars. . . . The German refining industry employs,

spread over upwards of fifty establishments, a large capital (3,000,000 florins), invested in buildings, fixtures, and stock. The *sad results obtained* on an average from these institutions *during the last few years, threaten this capital with annihilation.'* And again, further on : 'The condition of German sugar refineries has been for a long time, not only an unfavourable one, but, indeed, *has declined from year to year.'*

Lastly, we come to Austria. Our Secretary, Mr. Jerningham, reports: 'The drawbacks allowed hitherto, instead of remaining that which they were intended, viz., a true return of the excise duties, have in reality proved Bounties to the manufacturers; and the history of sugar taxation is that of the struggle of the Government to remedy this.' The system of assessment was necessarily at fault, and encouraged fraudulent practices. Matters came to a crisis in 1876, when it was discovered that on the system in vogue, Government paid 947,000 florins in drawbacks on sugar exported, and which had only paid 931,000 florins duty and taxes. Government has consequently interfered in self-defence of its own revenue, and ordained that eventually sugar is to pay annually a contribution to the revenue of 10,000,000 florins. This revenue argument is thus one of immense cogency. The Belgian Government have similar experience ; they know that some two million francs more revenue ought and could be obtained from sugar, but that this now finds its way into the pockets of the growers, because of the insuperable difficulties of collection wherever sugar is concerned. Russia is in similar evil plight.

But the success of the Austrian growers and refiners at the expense of their country, has in its course roused and frightened other nations. Thus, M. Jacquemont, speaking on behalf of French sugar manufacturers, after describing these results in Austria, recommends, on behalf of France, ' That in all treaties of commerce which may be negotiated, measures be taken to suppress Bounties on export generally. If not, we may expect to see our *great agricultural industry succumb in this struggle,* so strangely unequal, which it sustains, not only against rival industries, but against the revenues of the different European States.'

And it may be noted incidentally that this action of the Austrian Government will have the effect of almost doing away with the asserted outside effect of the Bounty; for, if we judge by the present state of the industry as pointed out by M. Jacquemont, 'If the proportion of the exportation to the total production should diminish, the Bounty would increase; if, on the contrary, the proportion should increase to 60 or 70 per cent. of the total production, the Bounties would decrease.' Thus, the case in Austria is at the present moment eminently favourable to English refiners and growers.

It would thus appear that in one and all the countries that now give Bounties there is a strong desire, on the part both of Government and of manufacturers, to abolish any Bounties on the exportation of sugar, whether raw or refined.

It is remarkable to trace in the history of the negotiations to put an end to Bounties that have already taken place between the Governments interested, that they have invariably originated in the desire of these Governments to remedy defects in their own financial arrangements. The advantage to the sugar industries was merely incidental, and, indeed, only brought to the light of day by the sugar manufacturers and refiners themselves.

It is also remarkable to notice that in all these

countries where Bounties are gained, the sugar industries are in a precarious condition; refining
dwindles where Bounties exist, while it is on the
increase in England. Growers of beet all the Continent over declare themselves ruined by the Bounty-
fed competition of each other. It is, therefore,
exceedingly remarkable to find so many of the wit-
nesses before the Commission, 'interested in sugar,'
so persistently, in the face of the figures they have
themselves produced, declaring that refining must
die out in England. It was shown them that,
on their own calculations, the Bounties received
annually in England was so many million pounds
sterling; that every few years these Bounties paid
into England as much capital as all that invested
in English sugar industries: that thus, even supposing the Bounties did destroy the industry, nevertheless they would have paid for both capital and
'good-will' over and over again.

§ 4. It is, then, evident that all the countries interested are anxious to do away with these Bounties.
There are but two methods of procedure desirable.
The one is the freeing of sugar from all connection
with the Exchequer. This has been accomplished in
England; but it is not within the range of 'practical
politics' that this should be accomplished in many,

still less in all, of the States that at present, in spite of themselves, grant Bounties.

We are compelled, then, to fall back upon the second and less satisfactory of the two desirable methods—that of manufacturing and refining in bond. Here again we find much happy unanimity arising among the various Governments interested. When this remedy was broached years ago there were many more or less idealistic objections put forward, on the score of the evils of direct Government interference in industrial details. Some evils are, however, necessary evils. Taxation itself is one of these; and it is not altogether illogical to infer that the collection of taxes should follow suit in this respect. But even in France refiners themselves have withdrawn their objections, and chiefly by reason of the experience there gained since 1852 by the manufacturing in bond of beet sugar. On this point the authorised evidence of M. Georges is conclusive:—

'Ques. 4047.—In the opinion of the fabricants in France is the refining in bond the only efficient mode of abolishing bounties?' 'Yes; it is the sole one, in their opinion. For ten years past they have been soliciting this measure. At the Trade Congress, at

Brussels, they passed a resolution that refining in bond was the only means of abolishing bounties.'

M. Fouquet handed in to the Committee the joint agreement entered into by the refiners and the fabricants of France advocating refining in bond.   Already, in Austria, the excise authorities test sugar, supervise in the factories, and examine books.   The factory-owner is required by law to provide accommodation for these officers.   The Austrian Government and the fabricants are thus already working without trouble a system of Government inspection, which involves more interfering than even the refining in bond calls for.   But after all has been said to show the desirability of refining in bond, there remains the difficult task of realizing the proposal.   And the apparent difficulty hinges on the desire or demand that any action in the matter must be action accepted and joined in by all the sugar-growing States.   Here again crops up the great difficulty of all general international action — the absence of what in law would be termed the sanction.   There is need of a common compelling power.

The decision has now been come to that a Conference of the Powers interested will have no good issue, unless they meet on the understanding that they will create some sanction as a common defence of themselves against those who may elect not to join such a convention as may be agreed upon. It has, therefore, been suggested that the Powers joining such a Conference shall agree beforehand to the insertion of a 'Penal Clause.'

Of what nature is this clause to be? The French Government maintains that it should impose a specific duty on any sugar imported from the recalcitrant country or countries. It has, indeed, been held that the mere insertion, or even intention to insert such a clause, will accomplish the desired effect, and scare all the Powers interested into joining the Convention. For an English Government, however, to assent to such a clause is simply impossible in the present temper of the English people. They will not impose fresh import duties for any other than revenue purposes. The English people are happily well aware of the prosperity and growth that has followed on their definite adoption of free trade principles; and to go back to interferences with trade for industrial purposes is a retrograde step that is happily an impossibility in the England of to-day.

There is another penal clause that is worthy

of mention, and that is the declining to receive
sugar from the erring State. This would be a
specially powerful weapon in the hands of England. It would encounter many difficulties—such
as those that cluster round 'certificates of origin';
—but both as a threat and as a check it would
in all probability have much direct success. Concerning the principles on which it is founded, it
is no doubt an interference with the free course
of trade, but we are working for concert with
Powers that follow a policy of protection. We
do not levy a duty; we do not seek or obtain
revenue; there is nothing fiscal in the whole arrangement; it is merely, as it were, joining in the
concerted blockade of a nation that is generally
felt to be acting contrary to the best interests of
all. Such a clause has the merit of assured effi-
cacy, if of nothing else. But it is a measure of
warfare and not of peace.

The question remains, what have we left we
can trust to in the absence of a penal clause? We
have, on the one hand, the welcome fact that all
the nations interested are in favour of establishing the manufacture and refining in bond. The
history of previous sugar conferences is the history
of the elimination of objections to such united

action. In 1862 attention was drawn to the fact that the various arrangements of drawbacks and duties on sugar were practically Bounties. Each country soon saw the error of its ways, and expressed its intention to do away with Bounties. But the one great obstacle was the fact that other countries might continue in their independence. The Conference in 1862-1863, was occupied in the main on the futile search for some method of exactly measuring percentages of sugar, either raw or refined. The standard of colour was adopted; and the consequent greater exactness certainly reduced the effect of the Bounty system. But it was soon seen that colour was no reliable test of strength; not only was it liable to 'manipulation,' fraudulent or otherwise, but sugars from different countries and of the same strength are often differently coloured; and again, sugars of the same colour are often of different strengths.

These, and other practical obstacles arose, and gave rise to fresh Conferences — each of them a step in the right direction. By the year 1872 a fresh Conference was proposed, in which the British delegates were instructed to ask for refining in bond. Nothing came of that Conference save a recommendation for further investigation.

The following year, 1873, another Conference was held; and at this, 'saccharimetry' of a highly scientific type was proposed as a method of deter-mining with all-sufficient accuracy the relative per-centage of sugar in the raw material. England this time withheld her consent.

The Conference in 1875 led to the Convention of that year which was to establish refining in bond in France and Holland. Holland withdrew on the plea of a misunderstanding as to her re-tention of her liberty at any time to abolish her sugar duties altogether. France then defended herself by establishing Saccharimetry.

Next followed the Paris Conference of 1876. At this conference Saccharimetry was carefully inquired into and declared finally to be a failure. The Conference eventually suspended its sittings without any agreement having been arrived at, in order to report to the respective Governments, with a view to the subsequent resumption of the Con-ference, to which it was proposed to invite Austria, Germany, and Italy. This Conference was resumed, but the three new States declined to send dele-gates: and eventually, after the fashion of its pre-decessors, it separated without visible effect.

During these eighteen years of effort much

advance was, however, made. The Dutch and the
French Governments declared in favour of refining
in bond, and the other sugar-producing countries
were invited to join. Moreover, the first motion
was then made towards discussing Bounties on raw
as well as on refined sugar. The Governments
of Italy and of Austria are in favour of abolishing
Bounties. These are new developments; and yet
there still remains the hard task of prevailing on
these various States to carry out in combination
what each one individually desires to see realized.

§ 5. England comes to a new Conference with clean
hands. She has taken what is admittedly the very
best course; she has suppressed sugar duties altogether. And in her hands she wields the powerful
lever of the recorded success attending on this
move. Our very sugar refiners, despite the real
effects of bad times and low prices, and despite
the more supposititious effects of Bounties, are doing
far better than the refiners of these Bounty-pro-
tected States. We continue to make use of more
and more raw sugar, to consume more and more
sugar. But we also export more and more refined sugar; and we also import less and less
refined sugar. The very latest figures are those
for the first five months of 1881; it is well to

put these side by side with those of the last two
years :—

	The first five Months in		
	1879.	1880.	1881.
Refined Sugar Imported from the Continent ...... }	723,000 ...	617,000 ...	575,000 = − 148,000 tons.
ii. Refined Sugar Imported from France .... }	47,000 ...	31,000 ...	28,000 = − 19,000 „
iii. Refined Sugar Exported from England .... }	197,000 ...	167,000 ...	203,000 = + 6,000 „

French refiners in these respects are stationary,
and Dutch and Belgian actually retrogressing. Our
West Indian producers also continue to increase
their output; and these facts give the lie to the
supposition that Bounty-fed beet-growing is or can
be in any way successful in supplanting the cane-
growing of the tropics.

It is in these facts that England has her most
powerful argument — her one great lever. We
could even contemplate the substitution for the
troublesome penal clause, in a convention of this
example, of the pre-eminent success of England's
freed production of sugar, both raw and refined.
So may England, in years to come, bring the
Bounty-giving States to see that, while they discover that Bounties injure their own native industries, and become a terrible drag on their own
exchequers, yet that these Bounties are quite
incapable of making anything like a ' disastrous

impression' on the 'Home and Colonial Sugar Industries of this Country,' for the reason that these industries in the British Empire are free of the baneful incubus of the Bounty system. With these facts in our pockets we may safely face negotiations for a new convention; we may trust, even if with hope rather than with confidence, that other Governments will in due course pay heed to their experience in their own exchequers, and to the unanimous opinions of their own sugar growers and refiners, as to the deleterious influence of the Bounty system, and that they will follow the successful lead of England in removing all that in any way directs or restricts industrial energy and deprives it of its essential liberty to follow its natural bent.

CHAPTER V.

PROTECTION IN YOUNG COMMUNITIES.

§ 1. Parallel cases of Victoria and New South Wales.　§ 2. The Promotion of Manufactures.　§ 3. The Raising of Revenue. § 4. The Promotion of General Prosperity.　§ 5. Value of this test case.

§ 1. JOHN STUART MILL has told us that Protection, altogether demolished as a general principle, might be found *under certain conditions* economically defensible in a young community. This hypothetical concession on Mill's part has had a direct and practical effect on the commercial policies adopted in some States—notably in one or two of our own Colonies and in the United States. But Mill in this argument expressly declares he is only dealing with what might be, and that the whole argument only applies, provided certain conditions come to be realized. Professor Sumner, of Yale, one of the ablest economists in the United States, well sums up the point in the words, " In these, as in other matters, we cannot argue with certainty from what might have been." Both he and Mill regret the absence of recorded facts on this point of Protection in Young Communities.

Recent experiences enable me in some measure to make good this deficiency, and to fill up this gap in the experiential foundations of Political Economy, with what, for all practical purposes, is a test case. For this purpose I simply summarise facts recorded in authoritative official records.

The history for the past ten years of our two great Colonies of Victoria and New South Wales provides us with the necessary records. This is the first time in history that we meet with the story, told in the details of actual fact, of two young communities growing up side by side with practically similar economic environments and opportunities, but pursuing the one a Free Trade and the other a Protectionist policy. In Victoria, in the year 1865, Sir J. Mac-Culloch introduced a modified form of Protection, and since 1871 there has prevailed that very intensified form of which the late Premier, Mr. Graham Berry, has been the persistent advocate. Over this same period, and more especially since 1874, New

I

South Wales has followed an essentially Free Trade course.

It may be added that I had the good fortune to sojourn in these Colonies in the year 1870, and again in the year 1878. This implies the advantage of personal and local experience of the two Colonies, and of the two Colonies at two periods separated by an appropriate interval of eight years.

So far as the purpose in hand is concerned, these two Colonies were in the year 1870 sufficient counterparts of each other in regard to economic environments and opportunities. Either community may be described as a pioneer band of the great English nation, engaged in opening up virgin lands rich in all natural wealth. Our fellow-countrymen in Victoria and in New South Wales had provided for themselves all the aids and advantages our present civilisation offers. Roads, railways, telegraphs, postal arrangements, sea communications, education, and so forth, were all in a high state of perfection. All the facilities of life under the care of energetic administrations had developed with marked rapidity. At the same time these two Colonies yield to no country in the world in the richness of their natural endowments. Both above and below ground the soil is pregnant with wealth; and the climate is all

Englishmen can desire for the due exertion of their productive energies. Thus in these two Colonies the scientific industry of this nineteenth century had found its most favourable opportunities.

In the nature of things, these two Colonies are, for the present, producers mainly of raw material which they exchange for the manufactured products of more populous centres. Thus we find the inhabitants of these Colonies import twice as much value per head as the inhabitants of the British Islands. This is a fact of much value to our present purpose. The United States have been perpetually put forward in the Free Trade controversy. But the United States only import a value of 2*l*. per head of population per annum. We in these British Islands import, say, 10*l*. per head. But in these two Colonies the imports are, in value, 20*l*. per head of population per annum. Consequently, the direct effect of high or low tariffs is ten times as great in these instances as in that of the United States, and the value of these instances ten times as great to the economist.

The necessary starting-point of the comparison is the determination that at the beginning of the decade these two young communities were the sufficient counterparts of each other in regard to economic environments and opportunities. The

Protectionists of Victoria offer justification or apology for their swerving from the straight course pursued by New South Wales on the three pleas of lesser extent of territory, larger population, and absence of coal.

In regard to this *lesser extent of territory*, we find that Victoria has sold 11,000,000 acres, and has 45,000,000 still unsold; and that New South Wales has sold 33,000,000 acres, and has still 165,000,000 acres unsold. In each case the State has sold, or in other words has settled, from one-fourth to one-fifth of its area. In each case there remain over three-fourths of the area open for settlement. At present the population to the square mile in Victoria is ten persons, and in New South Wales three persons. In the United Kingdom the proportion is 270. Both Colonies are thus only on the threshold of their career as populated and developed countries. There is the real difference that the *future* capabilities of New South Wales are greater. But the present case refers solely to the *past* ten years. And during that decade the extent of the unoccupied lands is not so much to the point as the fact that in either case there are three-fourths of the soil of the Colony still open for settlement. In each Colony men are pushing on with their flocks and their herds to occupy new areas of virgin soil, and the plough follows in their track to pioneer agricultural settlement. In neither case has this operation as yet advanced over the whole. That is the condition at the present; and we are dealing with the past, and not with the future.

In regard to the *larger population of Victoria,* that also is a relative matter. Each Colony is but sparsely populated. Victoria, the size of England, Wales, and Scotland combined, is at the present peopled by a population equalling that of Kent only. New South Wales is about three times the size of Victoria, with a somewhat smaller population. In either case, after deducting the quarter of the population that congregates in the capital of each Colony, we have but a very sparse and scattered population over the interior. It must be conceded, however, that in so far as the population of Victoria is relatively denser than that of New South Wales, in so far manufactures, or revenue, or prosperity, or growth should develop with greater natural speed in Victoria than in New South Wales; in so far as Victoria had a larger or a denser population than New South Wales, in so far Victoria started with superior natural or inherent advantages in those

very objects to foster which Victorians instituted
their policy of Protection.

In regard to the great superiority of New South
Wales in the production of *coal*, it is well to remember that this coal is produced on the Hunter
River, and has to be carried thence by sea to
Sydney, which is the centre of manufacturing
enterprise. It is well known that when once coal
has to be shipped the difference in length of voyage
of one day to Sydney or three days to Melbourne
makes but little difference in actual cost. So that
in the question of fuel for manufacturers there is
little practical difference in regard to coal supply
in the two Colonies. As a wealth-yielding force
against the *coal* of New South Wales must be set
off the great superiority of Victoria in the production of *gold*. It is true that the gold industry has
declined rapidly in Victoria in output, and in
number of men employed. But we must
remember there is also a gold-mining industry in
New South Wales which has also declined. This
decline is due to the fact that gold was first discovered in alluvial soil, disintegrated from the quartz
by the action of nature. Alluvial diggings provided
a rich harvest; but they soon became exhausted,
and miners had to turn to extracting the gold from

the primeval envelope of quartz. This led to a complete revolution in the mining industry. The falling off of the output in gold consequent on this revolution was not the annihilation of capital, nor was it the forcing labour to leave the Colony in search of employment. The city of Ballarat survived and continued to thrive as the great centre of the investment of capital in mining, which had superseded 'digging.' Quartz reefs had to be attacked instead of alluvial plains, and this change involved investment of more capital : powerful engines, colossal stamping machinery, and miles of tunnelled galleries and shafts had become necessary, and gold mining needed and absorbed a far greater amount of capital than in the old days when picks and shovels and wooden cradles were all the plant and implements requisite. Much of the very capital that the rich gold 'diggings' had yielded was at once invested in these new works. But there remained over much capital so accumulated which was not thus utilised, and which was there ready to start or promote any new industries.

Labour, too, was set free. In 1871 there were over 57,000 gold-miners in Victoria. By the year 1878 the number had dwindled to 37,000. This had set free in Victoria some 20,000 men of the artisan and mechanic class—of a class, too, which was originally recruited very largely from the manufacturing districts of the Old Country. There was thus provided during this decade, labour of a very applicable type for those very manufactories which were now to be fostered by Protection. Thus in this respect, in this very failure of the gold industry, Victoria gained over New South Wales in this supply of capital and of appropriate labour for those purposes for which the high tariff was imposed.

Besides this, the greater amount of gold obtained in Victoria had attracted at once a far larger population, and yielded forthwith much capital. This led to the fact that in Victoria, at the beginning of the decade under review, the railway system, and indeed all the facilities of life, had reached a higher stage of development than those of New South Wales. In every respect, then, we see that if there was any difference between the two Colonies ten years ago, it was a difference in favour of Victoria, so far as the starting manfactories, the affording revenue, or the promoting the general growth of prosperity were concerned. And these were the objects for which the high tariff was imposed.

In 1870, then, such were the relative economic positions of Victoria and New South Wales. What happened during the succeeding decade is set out in a variety of official documents and records, in greater part issued by the Victorian Government. These results range themselves conveniently under the heads—Manufactures, Revenue, General Prosperity and Growth.

§ 2. *Manufactures.* — When Protection speaks of fostering manufactures it speaks of fostering those industries which result in the production of commodities other than food and raw materials. And the plea is that, except for such fostering, these industries will be slow to arise in the community. Do we find justification of this in fact? The evidences are to be seen in the employments of the people and of capital; in the output of manufactured articles; and in the number and kind of manufactures developed.

In regard to the employment of the people, we find that at the end of the decade there were 25,000 persons making their living in manufactories in New South Wales, equivalent to 3·7 per cent. of the total population. In Victoria there were 28,000 persons so employed, equivalent to 3·2 per cent. of the larger population of that Colony. This so far disposes of the argument so often advanced that Protection promotes civilisation by providing civilised employment for the people in a new community.

Again, in Victoria during the decade, population had increased by one-eighth; but the number of hands employed in manufactures had increased one-third. Side by side with this we remember the very pertinent fact that the greater falling off in gold-mining had set free a large body of appropriate labour. There was this transference from one congenial occupation to another, but no development of any new class of operatives. By this transference of forces Victorian manufactures received an impetus totally unconnected with any fiscal or commercial policy.

Unfortunately the official records are in number of manufactories, and they afford no evidence of the size of the units so recorded. The number of foundries, clothing manufactories, agricultural implement and other works, has largely increased in both Colonies. So far as kind goes we find that as great a variety of manufactures has come into being under the low as under the high tariff. In either case the development as compared with the great natural industries of the country is insignificant. In one or two instances such industries have assumed larger dimensions in Victoria than in New South Wales. There are now, for instance, 750 hands employed in woollen manufacture in Victoria as compared with the 300 in New South

Wales. But then, to counterbalance this, we find one manufacturing industry which has grown up in the Free Trade and dwindled in the Protectionist Colony, and that is the important industry of shipbuilding. Ten years ago Victoria built 800 tons of shipping, and New South Wales built 1,800 tons. Now the annual output is only 400 tons for Victoria, while it has risen to 3,000 in New South Wales. Under the low tariff this important industry has doubled itself; under the high tariff it has diminished by one-half.

As an example of what is at present proceeding we have a report of its committee to the Association of the protected bootmakers at Melbourne, in which the following passage occurs :—" Our travellers report to us that they find very great difficulty in placing our goods on the neighbouring markets, *principally through the competition of Sydney with their own manufacture,* and European imported, sold sufficiently low to secure the custom. It must be remembered that Sydney has always had a steady export of her own manufactures, and that her *manufacturers* are giving inducements to our best workpeople to remove there. It also must be remembered *that all leathers*—the boot manufacturer's raw material—are admitted free into the port of Sydney, while an import duty of $7\frac{1}{2}$, 10, and 20 per cent. is enforced in Victoria, thereby placing the *Sydney manufacturer* at an advantage."

It is not easy, in the absence of definite records, to estimate the actual output from these manufactories, and in neither Colony is there any appreciable export of commodities locally manufactured. But if we compare the articles which are imported into Victoria under a heavy duty, and which enter New South Wales free, we shall find that, in spite of the increase in price, Victoria still is forced to supply herself with these ' prohibited ' or ' weighted' foreign articles ; and imports of these classes, on an annual average, about as much as the unprotected New South Wales.

Consequently, in regard to the development of manufactures in these new communities, we find there is not much difference in results between the Free Trade and the Protectionist policy if we look at the employment of people, output of manufactured articles, and number and kind of manufactures actually developed.

§ 3. *Revenue.* — Protection, especially for young communities, is over and over again defended on the plea that revenue must be raised. This plea is common with statesmen not only in one or two of our own Colonies, but in the United States. It is the great plea set up in Germany by the Bismarck party. This plea proceeds on the assumption that the higher the tariff the greater must be the revenue derived from the customs duties. Theoretical economists point out that "to tax your trade is to destroy your trade;" that "where Protection begins there Revenue ends;" that "to hamper the entry of goods into your market by heavy duties is to starve even unto death the goose that is to lay your golden eggs of Revenue." More practical economists hold that it is a mere question of balances, and that it is conceivable so cunningly to adjust the duties that, while inevitably destroying some of the trade existing under a lower tariff, this higher tariff yet sucks more revenue in the aggregate out of the lesser trade that remains. The question is really solved only by appeal to experience. And experience tells us that a low Customs' tariff yields most actual revenue. It appears, if we look to the records, that the annual revenue derived from the high tariff in the United States has fallen steadily during the last decade from thirty-seven to twenty-seven millions sterling. During the same period the English low tariff steadily contributed and still contributes an annual contribution to the revenue of twenty millions sterling. During the

decade the population of the United States has been
increased by ten millions of people, that of the
United Kingdom by only four millions.   So the
English people, with all the acknowledged advantages
of a low tariff, contribute, *pro ratâ*, actually more
revenue by the means of customs duties than the
citizens of the United States, who are hampered
by all the acknowledged evils of a high, a very
high tariff.

The recorded results over the same decade in
Victoria and New South Wales corroborate in a
striking manner this matter-of-fact conclusion.
During the decade the amount derived from customs
duties in New South Wales has gradually risen
from 950,000*l.* to 1,300,000*l.*   Over the same period
the high tariff has provided to the Victoria revenue
annual contributions which, if they have fluctuated
at all, have shown a downward tendency, and now
yield annually 1,400,000*l.*   It will be observed that
the smaller population of New South Wales contributes as much to the revenue by the means of its
low tariff as the larger population of Victoria contributes by means of its high tariff.   These are facts
and not fancies, and it is only by ignoring them or
being ignorant of them that any responsible authority
can put forward this revenue argument.

§ 4. *General Prosperity and Growth.*—I have said that Victoria and New South Wales each imports twice as much per head of population as we do in these islands. It is obvious that any policy which affects their imports must affect their general life and well-being to a degree unknown even in these commercial islands. And I pass to compare the two Colonies in regard to general prosperity and growth. The signs of this are external and internal; the signs are to be seen in their dealings with the outside world and also in their domestic condition.

Firstly, then, as regards their dealings with the outside world. This is a most significant index of their actual welfare, seeing that their external trade is double in value per head of population to what it is even in England. This trade is a sure indicator of prosperity, inasmuch as it is a sure indicator of any increase or decrease in consumption and pro- duction, the two visible factors of prosperity. Ten years ago New South Wales was doing an external trade of the annual value of 19,000,000*l.* A decade of steady increase brought this total up to 29,500,000*l.* in 1880. Ten years ago Victoria was doing an annual external trade of 27,600,000*l.* In the succeeding decade a wavering line of rise and fall brings us to an annual total of

30,500,000*l.* for 1880. Under the high tariff external
trade increased during the decade by one-ninth
only. Under the low tariff external trade increased
by more than one-half of its previous annual total.
The full significance of this is seen when we find
New South Wales, at the end of the decade, doing
10,000,000*l.* more annual trade than at the beginning, while Victoria was only doing some 3,000,000*l.*
more. Ten per cent. profit on such trade would
mean an addition to the annual national income of
New South Wales of 1,000,000*l.*, and to that of
Victoria only some 300,000*l.*

Incidentally it is worthy of note that the German
Government, perhaps the best informed Government
at present in existence, has chosen for the head-
quarters of its Consul-General for Australasia the
capital of the low tariff Colony, although the high
tariff Colony is at the present moment ahead in
number of population and in value of external trade.
The Germans evidently judge of the certain future
by means of the recorded past.

Further instruction follows on further analysis of
this external trade. If we turn to the exports we
find that ten years ago the value of articles, the
produce or manufacture of the Colony itself, was
exactly 77 per cent. of the total value exported from

each Colony. At the end of the decade we find the amount of this native produce exported had *risen* to 83 per cent. in New South Wales, but had *fallen* to 68 in Victoria. In other words, under the low tariff there had been increase, and under the high tariff decrease, in the exportable surplus of native products, a most important sign of prosperity and growth.

If we turn to the imports we find that ten years ago there entered New South Wales goods to the value of 9,000,000*l.* At the end of the decade this annual value had mounted to 14,000,000*l.*, an increase of 60 per cent. Ten years ago the imports into Victoria were of the value of 12,500,000*l.* At the end of the decade this annual value had mounted to 14,600,000*l.*, an increase of 20 per cent. only. In other words, not only the power but the using of the power to purchase foreign produce (and there was profit accruing to each purchase made) increased by about three times the speed under the low tariff to what it did under the high tariff.

There is another point in this external trade of much significance. In New South Wales there has been an increase in the tonnage of the shipping visiting the Colony during the decade, from 1,500,000 to 2,600,000 tons. In Victoria the increase has been from 1,300,000 to 2,200,000. It may be said that

K

this difference in growth is inevitable under a low as opposed to a high tariff, but it none the less represents a fountain of popular well-being, drawn upon in the one case to a much more profitable extent than in the other.

In connection with this shipping there are the very important records of ballast. There came to New South Wales during the decade 3,000,000 tons of shipping in ballast. There left New South Wales during the decade 117,000 tons of shipping in ballast. There came to Victoria during the decade 113,000 tons in ballast. There left Victoria 2,500,000 tons, the greater proportion of which proceeded to New South Wales. Empty ships *arriving* in New South Wales have increased from an annual tonnage of 220,000 in 1870 to a tonnage of 320,000 in 1880. Empty ships *leaving* Victoria have increased from an annual tonnage of 198,000 tons in 1870 to a tonnage of 250,000 in 1880.[1] It will be observed that the conditions are exactly reversed in favour of the growth of the low-tariff colony.

[1] The *Sydney Morning Herald*, in an able leader on my article, very properly suggests that some of this ballasting may be due to the fact that vessels freighted to Melbourne afterwards come on to New South Wales for coal. But the *Herald* points out that besides this Sydney is rapidly becoming the one mercantile centre of the Australian seas.

The domestic or internal condition and progress of these two Colonies will complete the illustrations we would give of their growth and prosperity.

In the first place, in regard to *population*, we find that that of New South Wales has increased from 520,000 in 1870 to 740,000 in 1880, an increase of 48 per cent. The population of Victoria has increased from 730,000 in 1870 to 860,000 in 1880, an increase of only 17 per cent. In the second place, in regard to *wealth*, already we have seen in every point we have touched upon the far greater rapidity with which wealth-producing developments have been proceeding in New South Wales than in Victoria. From this we infer the fact that wealth is being produced in similar ratio. And when we read that the value of rateable property has doubled in New South Wales in the decade, and only increased by one-half in Victoria, we have our inference signally verified by recorded facts.

Singular evidence is afforded, also, by the statistics of the Savings Banks. In New South Wales the deposits have increased from 930,000*l.* to 1,500,000*l.*; and the number of the depositors from 21,000 to 32,000. In Victoria the deposits have increased from 1,100,000*l.* to 1,600,000*l.*; but the depositors have increased in number from 38,000 to 76,000.

K 2

In other words, the average amount deposited has
risen in New South Wales steadily from 44*l.* per
head to 47*l.* In Victoria the average deposited per
head has fallen from 29*l.* to 15*l.* This is evidence
corroborating the fact so commonly asserted that in
democratic Victoria wealth is accumulating in the
hands of the few. This is a result generally asso-
ciated with a high tariff by all writers on political
economy. It is a result which, in its direct antagonism to the wholesome principle of equable
distribution of wealth, stamps it as one of the most
injurious results of a high tariff.

Illustrative of this tendency is the fact that the
average wages of skilled labour grew in New South
Wales, during the decade, from being lower to being
higher than similar wages in Victoria. That wages
should have risen under a low tariff faster than
under a high tariff is a fact of great importance,
especially to countries wherein manhood suffrage
gives to the wage-earner so much political power
and responsibility. But it is a fact of which most
people are ignorant.

It is well also to notice that the prices of the
necessaries of life—of wheat, tea, and provisions
and tools and implements—are generally lower in
New South Wales than in Victoria. This, of course,

adds much force to the before-recorded results in the nominal rates of wages, for it adds the essential element of greater relative purchasing power under the low tariff.

In order to form an exact estimate of social well-being we must build a general judgment on numerous details; and among these details marriages afford apposite information. In New South Wales during the decade the annual number of marriages has steadily increased from 3,800 to 5,100—an increase of one-third; in Victoria the increase in annual number has been from 4,700 to 5,100; an increase of one-eighth only. While in New South Wales marriages are in the proportion of 7 to every 1,000 of population; in Victoria they are but 6 per 1,000. And this is the more remarkable when we remember that in New South Wales there are 80 women to every 100 men, whereas in Victoria there are 90 women to every 100 men.

Ample details have thus accumulated during the past decade to show that in regard to all outward signs of prosperity and growth—social, industrial, commercial—the Colony with the low tariff has pro- gressed with far greater rapidity than the Colony with the high tariff. This exhibits the great prac- tical use of statistics. They are thus brought to substantiate, by the cold logic of recorded acts and facts, the reports and rumours that have been rife in these two Colonies. The newspapers, it is true, had provided from day to day pictures of New South Wales altogether devoid of the sombre economical colouring that had become the salient feature in the accounts of Victoria. Nor has there been in New South Wales that general outspoken discontent among capitalists as well as among working men which has from time to time manifested itself in Victoria. Under the high tariff each industrial class in Victoria has in its turn bitterly complained of the duties that specially weigh upon it. The latest information carries on the tale to deputations of miners demanding of Government a lowering of duties on imported mining machinery and tools. The farmers have been for some time threatening to give up their farming because of the high prices they are forced to pay for their implements and materials— high prices unknown over the border in the low tariff colony of New South Wales. Multitudes of labourers, the very men who by their votes supported the policy of "Protection" to native labour, have had from time to time to stave off starvation at relief-work wages. It has been for some time more than suspected that capital had set in a strong current towards other Colonies ; it was not, however, known that the current of labour, far less easily transferable, had set in the same direction. The skilful and conscientious estimates of population made from year to year by the Victorian Statistical Department, under the guidance of that very able statist Mr. Hayter, proved, when the actual records of the census of this year came to be taken, to be no less than 76,000 of people over the mark in a population of 850,000. Mistaken popular opinion refused to recognise the enormous emigration of labouring men *and their families* that had been proceeding all the while. But by this official recording of facts this popular error has now been set straight

§ 5. It is well, in conclusion, to summarise the general lessons of these recorded results. In his address to the Economic Section at the jubilee meeting of the British Association, Mr. Grant Duff put forward as a text the sentence, "Methods that answer follow thoughts that are true." This idea may be profitably amplified into the corollary, "Thoughts that are true follow knowledge of methods that do not answer." It has been my object to afford knowledge of methods that answer and also of methods that do not answer; and this knowledge has been sought in the recorded results of rival methods. This knowledge, when acquired, must be followed by thoughts that are true. In Victoria itself it is hoped this record of what has already taken place will give fresh impulse to the reactionary movement in favour of a lower tariff. Signs of this movement are already apparent. The new Premier, Sir Bryan O'Loghlan, has issued a Royal Commission to inquire into the working of the tariff, and he apologetically promises the people of Victoria 'a free breakfast-table.' These are thoughts that are true, and they seem to be following on the knowledge of methods that do not answer.

In the wider sphere of the British Empire these recorded results may stimulate local Parliaments to maintain low tariffs. We must look to the spread of sound knowledge and to the honest subordination of class interests to the common national good rather than to fostering duties on foreign wheat, if we would successfully set the great and growing commerce of the empire on sound and profitable economic foundations. Until the Canadian Dominion, for political rather than economic purposes, not long ago swerved from the right path, there was but one Colony, and that one the unfortunate Colony of Victoria, among the eight great self-governing Colonies enjoying independence of fiscal action, that had burdened itself with a high tariff. It would seem that Victoria has paid the penalty of its backsliding. That the others did not follow suit is plain evidence of the great practical common sense and public loyalty of the majority of British Colonists. To this and to the spread of knowledge of recorded results we may look for a continuance of this tendency towards low tariffs throughout the British Empire. This tendency, if persevered in, will enable every Englishman, no matter where he may be domiciled over the wide empire, to thrive on the fact which has done England itself such unbounded material good, that whatever he uses or consumes is obtained by him at the lowest possible cost. Such action is urgently recommended by economic science, for it must contribute to the material prosperity of every industrial worker throughout the whole British Empire.

CHAPTER VI.

ONE-SIDED FREE TRADE.

§ 1. Supposed necessity for Customs Duties.   § 2. Hong Kong growing and prosperous with no Customs Duties.   § 3. People increasingly employed in Arts of Civilization.   § 4. Ample Revenue raised.

§ 1. FOUR of the commonest pleas put forward in defence of the imposing a high tariff, at all events in Colonies, are—

(1.) We must have Revenue, and we can best get it by the means of customs duties.

(2.) Even Mill allowed there might be something to be said for protecting, by a high tariff, the industries of a rising community.

(3.) If you don't protect by customs duties, you will have a merely barbarous state—with no manufacturers, no civilized industries.

(4.) You must protect yourself by a high tariff when you have a much more populous neighbour rigidly protecting himself by a high tariff.

These are the pleas we have heard used by statesmen in Germany, Victoria, the United States, Canada,
and other places ; and we know they are pleas that
are acted up to.

I would call the attention of those who hold such
views for one moment to certain recorded results, in
which they will find ample food for reflection.

§ 2. I would ask them to consider the one instance
of Hong Kong. Here is a small community, intimate
neighbour to an empire which is out of all comparison more populous and which protects itself by every
means of restriction and exclusion. And yet this small
community is in a most flourishing condition; thriving
in all civilized industries, manufacturing much, and
contributing a sufficient revenue of 1*l.* 7*s.* per head of
inhabitants ;—although it levies no customs duties
whatever. These are recorded results that Protectionists everywhere should carefully weigh and
ponder over. I do not for one moment say that all
the prosperity of Hong Kong is due to her having no
customs duties. All I wish to point out is, that a
young community contributes a very large revenue,
and flourishes in all civilized prosperity, not even
omitting manufacturing industry, though it imposes
no customs duties whatever. It flourishes in all these
respects without the aid of that shield of Protecting

duties which Protectionists tell us is vitally essential. It flourishes in every way, though it pursues a policy of what some call 'one-sided Free Trade,' that is, about as one-sided as such a policy can well be.

Full details of all this happens to have been recently published in an Official Report, by the Governor, Sir John Pope Hennessy, on the condition of Hong Kong in the year 1876, and again in the year 1881. This official comparison is both suggested and rendered possible, because it so happens a census was taken in the year 1876, and again in 1881, when all the British Empire underwent the same process.

In the absence of a customs tariff, it is scarcely surprising to find trade and commerce increase at a rapid rate. Nor is it surprising to find a concomitant development in all the divisions of social growth. On the one hand we find that the boats used in the harbour for landing and transferring cargoes, which numbered 1,860 in the year 1876, had, by the year 1881, increased to a total of 2,780. There are four times as many steam launches in the latter as in the former year. And the Chinaman traders—the busy Hongs, who introduce English manufactures into China—and the various branches of money-lenders and local traders, and dealers, had risen in number, in five short years, from 1,200 to 4,000. It seems but natural to read after these figures, that in all details of social growth considerable and corresponding progress had taken place. For instance, during the last year to which the Report refers, Chinese had purchased landed properties in the Colony to no less an amount than 600,000*l.* This is a very surprising growth ; but Free Traders will only say of it that it was but to be expected.

And yet when we look further into details, we see much that must interest those who allow there is something in the four contentions mentioned at the commencement of this chapter. We find that the population had increased from 139,000 to 160,000, and that the increase was largely accounted for by an increase of 20,000 in the number of Chinese. Many of these were immigrants from China, and the remainder natural increase of previous arrivals, who preferred Hong Kong to China. And yet in China all industries are hedged round with a wall of Protection, to defend them from those breezes of free competition to which all industries in Hong Kong are so fully exposed.

§ 3. In each census elaborate details are given of the employment of the population. We may conveniently class these under four heads. *Commerce and Trade*, will include the Hongs, money-lenders,

dealers, traders, merchants, and all engaged in exchange—especially in such Chinese commodities as
birds-nests and joss-house requisites. *Manufacturing*
will include the numerous makers of innumerable
articles—of boats, cigars, glass, matches, sails, boxes,
lanterns, rifles, sauce, soap, spectacles, sugar, tooth-
powder, umbrellas, and vermilion. Among *mechanics
and artisans* we find carpenters, smiths (of all metals),
masons, rice-pounders, stone-cutters, and tailors.
And lastly, we have a large class more *intellectually*
employed as doctors, druggists, dentists, architects,
fortune-tellers, schoolmasters, portrait-painters, students, and photographers. Placed in a tabulated form
these records yield a significant lesson.

TABLE.

EMPLOYMENT OF CHINESE IN HONG KONG, 1876 AND 1881.

Employment.	No. in 1876.	Percentage of Total Population.	No. in 1881.	Percentage of Total Population.
Commerce	1,400	1	4,300	$2\,^7/_{10}$
Manufactures	980	$^6/_{10}$	1,490	$^9/_{10}$
Mechanics	7,080	$5\,^2/_{10}$	10,200	$6\,^5/_{10}$
Intellectual Occupations	1,060	$^7/_{10}$	3,240	2
TOTALS	10,520	$7^1/_2$	19,230	12

There has thus been a steady and large growth in the employment of the natives in the arts and industries of civilization. No doubt much of this is due to the particular encouragement given by a free port to commerce and shipping. We read, for instance, in the description of Hong Kong, given in the Colonial Office List : " Hong Kong is well provided with dock accommodation. There are five docks and three slips, which are well supplied with shears, engineers' and carpenters' shops, foundries, and every requirement for making large repairs to ships of war and merchant vessels." But if we add to the list the European adults, we shall find engaged in these and numerous other industrial and manufacturing works more than 20,000, in a total population of only 160,000. Such a result compares very favourably with what has been attempted in the Colony of Victoria in Australia for instance. There a high protective tariff has been set up, specially for the purpose of fostering manufactures, and yet we find that there only 56,000 people are employed in manufacturing industries out of a total population of 860,000, one for every 15. In Hong Kong, with no tariff whatever, and with an enormous densely populated protected country of similar race in close proximity, there are 12,000 people so employed out

of a total population of 160,000, one for every
13 of total population.   Thus not only in the
matter of prosperity but of employment as well
there exists a state of things in Hong Kong the very
reverse of what the advocates of Protection tell us
must occur in young communities unless they set
up protective customs tariffs.

§ 4. Another class of theorists, many of whom arro-
gate to themselves the functions and fame of statesmanship, tell the world "We leave to academic
political economists this question of high, low, or no
tariffs; we are concerned with every-day life; we have
to raise revenue; and our academic friends involved
in the clouds of abstract theory will not condescend
to allow us the means of raising revenue." Many
have said and written, that customs duties, and high
customs duties too, are absolutely necessary in Colonies, for the purpose of raising the necessary revenue.
And yet we find Hong Kong, like the Colony of the
Straits Settlement, successfully raising a very considerable and an elastic revenue, without the aid of
any customs duties whatever.   I do not for one
moment advance this in evidence as to the universal
and absolute condemnation of customs duties, but
merely as proof, by recorded results, that revenue
can be raised, and successfully and abundantly raised,

in their absolute absence. The following short table exhibits clearly the relative Revenues derived from taxation in four of our Colonies, per head of population :—

	Revenue. £	Population.	Revenue Per Head. £ s. d.
Victoria—High Tariff . . .	1,700,000	... 850,000	... 2 0 0
New South Wales—Low Tariff.	1,400,000	... 720,000	... 1 19 0
Hong Kong—No Tariff . . .	221,000	... 160,000	.. 1 7 0
Straits Settlements—No Tariff.	366,000	... 270,000	... 1 7 0

When we remember that the Straits Settlements and Hong Kong have little or no interest to supply on any public debt but that both Victoria and New South Wales are considerably burdened in this respect, we shall see that these two free ports obtain ample revenue without resort to customs duties.

It is often supposed that Hong Kong can afford to do without customs duties, because of her rich opium monopoly. It is therefore worth while noticing that the opium taxation only yields one-fifth of the total Revenue. The bulk is derived from licences of various kinds and stamps, house-duty, and sundry small fees. And, after all, this opium revenue is 40,000*l*., from a population of 160,000, or 5*s*. per head ; and the revenue from tobacco in England is 8,000,000*l*., from a population of 34,000,000, or as nearly as possible the same amount per head. An adequate

L

revenue is raised without appeal either to customs duties or income-tax; and the experience of Hong Kong is, so far, a recorded result of the highest value, no less to the practical statesman than to the student of political economy.

The four objects mentioned at the beginning of this chapter ;—the raising of Revenue; the starting industries; the promotion of the arts of civilization in a young community; and the defending a young community of small size against the overwhelming influences of a mighty Protectionist neighbour ;—are found, in the recorded case of the recent growth of Hong Kong, to be obtainable without the aid of any customs tariff whatever. This is a lesson which may well and wisely be taken to heart by many statesmen, not only of our own Colonies but of the United States, and even of the Mother country as well—and it is a lesson which should be specially valuable to those who talk and write so much on the subject of " One-sided Free Trade."

CHAPTER VII.

A LOW TARIFF EMPIRE.

§ 1. Our Trade with our Colonies is growing faster than our Foreign Trade, and more steadily. § 2. We are not as yet properly alive in England to the importance of securing this New Trade. § 3. We are the only nation that does not endeavour to secure Free Trade within its own frontiers. § 4. We have several Classes of Colonies—all of which would profit by Intra-National Free Trade. § 5. The several Colonies should unite with England in spontaneously agreeing to keep their tariffs low. § 6. Then they need not fear outsiders, but will one and all secure their own highest prosperity.

§ 1. It is commonly acknowledged that since its adoption of the principles that now regulate its commercial policy, the English nation has enjoyed forty years of unexampled growth and prosperity. But what is not so often acknowledged is the equally important fact that the nation in this prosperous development has appropriated vast unoccupied tracts of the earth's surface ; and that these appropriations, which, not many years ago, were penal settlements,

struggling whaling stations, or distant trading factories, have now grown into communities, whose
wealth, success, and importance already give them
claim to take rank among the prominent States
of the earth.

This rapid growth of the oversea portion of our
Empire is at the present moment silently but surely
making its weight felt in the most important
interests and works of the nation. Among these
none holds so important a place as the interchange
of the products of industry. Natural and human
forces exist in so vast a variety of combinations that
each country seems always able to supply to every
other country some definite products at a profit;
and it is on this natural exchange that the progress
of the human race in prosperity seems to depend.
These forces at present at work in England make us
produce a large surplus of manufactures. And if we
cannot sell this surplus, so much of our labour is
in vain, and the product of so much of our energy
absolutely valueless. What we must have is access
to outside markets. But if we sell in markets in
other communities we can only do so by obtaining
access on terms settled by these other communities,
and often dictated by considerations which have
but little relation to commercial or even to economic

needs. The terms of this access in Holland not so long ago, and in France at the present moment, depend rather on the political strategy of ministries than on the economic advantages of the nations concerned.

And yet our export manufacturers are putting forth all their vigour to prevent a rise in the French tariff. Our whole manufacturing body freely and liberally support the efforts and expenditure of our Foreign Office in its endeavours to keep low on the European continent the "price of access to continental markets." England spares no effort and no expense to maintain this established "custom." But up to the present, England has paid only too little heed to a new "custom," springing up in unlooked-for directions, a new "connection" which bids fair year by year to rival and to supplant this older connection.

Probably few of our manufacturers are aware of the following recorded results :—

TABLE I.

VALUE OF ENGLISH MANUFACTURES EXPORTED TO

	Europe.	Other Foreign Countries.	Our Colonies.
1870 . .	£54,600,000	£34,600,000	£44,200,000
1880 . .	52,400,000	32,900,000	58,500,000
	Decrease £2,200,000 ·	Decrease £1,700,000	*Increase* £14,300,000

TABLE II.

VALUE OF TOTAL TRADE OF UNITED KINGDOM WITH

	European Neighbours.*	Other Foreign Countries.	Our Colonies.
1873	. £157,000,000	£373,000,000	£152,000,000
1877	. 150,000,000	332,000,000	165,000,000

Decrease £7,000,000   Decrease £41,000,000   *Increase* £13,000,000

* France, Belgium, Holland, and Sweden and Norway.

From these two tables we learn two lessons. The first is that our own Colonies are growing into markets not only already equalling in magnitude the older established markets of other lands, but possessed of the further admirable attribute of unlimited future growth. *Our trade with France is practically stationary; our trade with our Australian Colonies by itself already equals our trade with France.* With France we have no reasonable prospect of a larger trade, because France is fully peopled and fully developed. With Australia our prospects of increased trade are commensurate with the fact that in Australia we have a continent capable by its own inherent fertility of supporting in prosperity a population of 200,000,000 human beings, and at present yielding wealth to a bare 3,000,000 of human workers. We make every effort to secure access to the dwindling French market: we make no public or appreciable effort to secure access to this real "market of the future" that invites us in Australia.

And what holds true of France and of Australia holds true of the whole of Europe contrasted with the whole of our Colonial Empire. In Europe we have a market old-established indeed, but in communities themselves fully developed, and moreover of natural and human forces very similar to those of our own islands. In our Colonies we have all this new grand possibility of markets (of which we have an earnest in their present rapid growth) in communities differing essentially in the character of their natural and human forces ; and therefore of far more certain value in the natural interchange of products of industry and enterprise. The Australian continent is overrun to grow wool, but its sparse workers in such industries congregate only reluctantly with sufficient concentration to produce conditions favourable to the genesis of the industries that find favour with the close-packed population of these islands. The areas we occupy in the tropics, where white labour is impossible, can be our allies but never our rivals. They can supply us with cotton and with sugar. But it will require a new civilization, a new order of mankind, to enable them to make for themselves machinery or even clothes on terms that can at all compete with the human vigour and the applicable mineral resources these islands possess.

Nor is it only of trade between England and the
Colonies that cognisance is being forced upon us.
There exists also a rapidly growing inter-colonial
commerce already of vast dimensions. The tonnage
of the shipping employed in this trade alone already
excels that of France and Germany added together.
The great Australian tea-market is now being largely
supplied from Ceylon and Assam. The very life
of some of our West Indian Colonies depends on
the fact that ships bring them continual supplies
of labour from India. As the British Empire grows,
so is it proved that *the mainspring of its prosperity
is free intercourse between its parts.*

The second table supplies us with a second lesson,
significantly witnessing to these things. We see in
this table the recorded effect of commercial depression on our trade. The Colonies record a protest,
and no mean protest, in our own favour. During
the four years of depression immediately succeeding
to that notorious period of inflation culminating in
the year 1873, we find our trade with our Colonies
continued to increase to the amount of 11 per cent. :
we find our trade with foreign countries *continued to
decrease* to the amount of 11 per cent. If we pay
heed to it, we have here an invaluable hint as
to the compensating influences resulting from width

of area and diversity of forces, both natural and human, provided their individual energies contribute in mutual union.

§ 2. The surface of the world, so far as Englishmen are concerned, is held by two classes of communities; the one class altogether independent one of another in sentiment and kinship, and only held together in any kind of forbearing union by the selfish interests of each individual community. The second class is a whole made up of homogeneous parts bound to one another by the powerful ties of national character and sentiment, as well as by the selfish interests of each individual community. This former class presents a mere discrete agglomeration of Foreign States; the latter class embraces the wide-spreading provinces of the British nation. The one class Englishmen seem to be able to affect only by the means of threats and destructive retaliation; the other class is directly ruled and controlled by Englishmen.

It needs to insist upon the strange fact, that while England is maintaining at great effort a precarious and utterly untrustworthy commercial connection with foreign states, the average public seems doggedly to shut its eyes to the opportunities afforded by England's extensive empire. It is true this unaccountable error disappears when we look to that main but silent current of industrial endeavour, which runs its course, fed by every streamlet and font of individual interest and enterprise, consistently in the true direction of success. This current has long ago recognised that within the frontiers of its own empire the lively productive enterprise of the English race has plenty of scope for the profitable exercise of all its powers : there are long years, long centuries of work, before these ample resources shall be, all of them, opened out. The Australias, by themselves, are equal in area and in natural capacity to the whole of Europe. In the Canadas and the districts of South Africa the English race possesses yet another potential Europe. And in India and the various tropical Colonies the nation possesses surface and wealth of resources equalling those of Europe. *The nation owns, then, an extent of surface and a variety of natural resources equal to three Europes conjoined.* Here then we have a field not altogether insufficient for employing the best energies of a nation of 50,000,000 people, and for providing unlimited scope for an unlimited increase of this nation.

Mr. Neufchatel in *Endymion* makes the appropriate and wise remark, " We do not want measures ; what we want is a new channel." At the present moment our manufacturers and our exporters want for their relief not measures but new channels; and trade, if we look to figures, is endeavouring to carve for itself a new channel in the mutual supplying of our wide empire. The great engine to the successful development of a vast mine of rich natural endowments is assured freedom of exchange. Labour and capital, energy and enterprise, skill and abstinence— these bases of successful production must be assured their opportunities of exertion over this vast field. In such case, and in such case alone, there opens out for Englishmen a new future of signal prosperity.

But the fact is that although England enjoys free trade, Englishmen do not. There is free trade in Great Britain; there is free trade in the Britsh Isles. But there exists also a greater Britain; there are British Isles, ay, and British continents, over the Atlantic and the Pacific, that at the present have not the assured advantage of free trade, and thus every moment run the risk of a relapse to the evils of fettered production and fettered exchange. It is undoubtedly true that the British Empire is, in itself, for the next century or so at all events, a complete world of production and consumption. But it is a world which does not at the present enjoy that true commercial union which insures freedom both of

exchange and of production. And yet it is a world
so circumstanced that it may, immediately if it will,
institute for itself the undoubted benefits of such
union; for it is a world inspired at the present by
the two essential bases of human union, community
of material interests and community of national
spirit.

§ 3. The very prime question in the whole matter
is the reason why there is not this free trade. And
the answer is simple. Under present conditions any
'self-governing' Colony finds itself free to adopt a
policy of protection if it will. Consequently English
merchants, manufacturers, or producers, no matter
where they may 'build their castles within the
Queen's dominions,' have at the present no guarantee
that they shall enjoy freedom of exchange in regard
to other portions of these same dominions. This is a
statement that can be made of no other nation past
or present, and it states a condition of things diame-
trically contrary to all accepted principles of national
union.

It was a quarrel about duties that caused us the
irreparable loss of the United States. And the very
first action taken by the citizens of the New Republic
was solemnly and irrevocably to institute perfect
freedom of exchange within the frontiers of their

own new empire. Within those frontiers customs
duties are to this day an impossibility. This eminently wise resolution has been one main element in
the growth and prosperity of the United States. In
all ages so soon as and whenever industry and commerce win for themselves a supremacy in the face of
politics and war, at once extended freedom of commercial intercourse is sought as an essential to existence. A Customs Union was the first sign of a
modern German nation. The jealous 'national
independence' of the petty German states in the
early years of this century soon discovered the fact
that free interchange of products was the one great
mutual interest none could afford to forego.

Moreover, at the present moment, if we look to
foreign nations, we see everywhere signs of a tendency towards 'customs union.' Italy is straining
every nerve, by the curious means of an elaborate
reciprocity, to bind up as many nations as possible
in close intercourse with herself. Belgium and
Holland, and also Austria and Germany, are con-
templating closer customs union. The United States
is eager to obtain secured commercial footing in
Europe. Spain is in earnest struggle to adjust the
commercial connections of her colonial empire.

Thus the English nation stands at the present

moment in a very singular position. It is an anomalous and a self-contradictory position, but yet one of those that recur in the history of nations that grow, and are not manufactured. The thoroughly English principle of self-government has now developed to such perfection in the larger provinces of the English Empire, that the fiscal policy of each province is regulated by the local Parliament. But this development has had an unlooked-for, an unexpected issue.

There have arisen cases in provinces where this self-government rules, in which the fiscal liberty has run to seed, and become fiscal licence. The consequence is that what was originally a grant or concession of liberty to the individual has threatened, in these latter days, to become a liberty that is destructive of the same liberty granted to the other individuals.

It seems to me that so long as this nation remains a nation it is not only its interest, but its paramount duty, to see that the liberty of any of its component parts be not in any way infringed by the action of other parts. Moreover, the fiscal liberty originally granted was merely and simply the handing over, for geographical reasons, to each separated community of Englishmen their right to devise and supply

the means to their own local government. To use this
liberty for other purposes, such, for instance, as the
discouraging the importation of particular products
from some other English community, seems to me a
direct subversion of this liberty, a distinct breach of
the grounds on which the nation made the concession. And the proof of this is the fact that the
using of it for these other unforeseen purposes at
once interferes with the grant of this liberty to the
other English communities.

Earl Russell in one of his speeches about the time
of these concessions, distinctly acknowledged this
principle :—

" With regard to our colonial policy, I have already
said that the whole system of monopoly is swept
away. What we have in future to provide for is that
there shall be no duties of monopoly in favour of one
nation and against another, and that there shall be
no duties so high as to be prohibitory against the
produce and manufacture of this country."

Earl Russell, with penetrating foresight, saw the
high commercial value our Colonies were to be to us.
And yet Canada has set up a high tariff, shutting
out some of our products ; and Victoria has done the
same. It is, however, *satisfactory to bear in mind*

that of our eight self-governing Colonies, only these two have as yet stepped aside from the right path. Canada, however, proffers the somewhat valid excuse of special necessities, bred of her political contiguity to a 'foreign' state of peculiar commercial views, and Canada has taken the lead in demanding free trade for all within the Empire. Victoria has no excuse but the fact that a crude but specious theory commends itself for the present to a majority of her manhood-suffrage rulers.

The awkward question remains, why, when with self-government the nation conceded the obvious addition of fiscal liberty *so far as the raising of revenue was concerned,* the nation did not rigorously watch that any other fiscal action, which in any way curtailed the liberties of other sections of the nation, and *for purposes other than revenue,* should have been allowed or disallowed as a totally distinct question.

§ 4. To the practical politician the interest centres in some adequate remedy: for the evil is accomplished: and any analysis of its demerits and its causes is only of use so far as it enlightens us in regard to its removal.

Inadequate information or thought leads many to forget that an authority still exists supreme over all others within the Empire. It is, indeed, only under

the shield of this central authority that the various
self-governing provinces enjoy this liberty to govern
themselves. But these various self-governing bodies
are constitutionally subordinate to the Imperial
Parliament; the true explanation of their virtual
independence is the fact that the Parliament has
delegated, for the sake of obvious expediency, some
of its powers to certain bodies of Englishmen, segre-
gated by long distances of 'disassociating' ocean.
But the natural tie of supremacy remains ; sanctioned
by the indisputable fact of the far greater material
and human power congregated in the centre of the
Empire ; and illustrated both by the eager willingness of the mother-country, on the first suspicion of
danger, to spare no exertion to render adequate
assistance to her oversea provinces, as well as by
the wise habit of colonial statesmanship to look to
the St. Stephen's Parliament for political inspiration
and guidance.

Nevertheless self-government, implying self-sup-
porting government, involves self-taxation, and so
the self-adjustment of fiscal policies. Each community of Englishmen may tax themselves how they
will to maintain their community in its corporate
concerns; but *to strain fiscal policies beyond the mere
maintenance of government is a course of action legal*

M

*only on the condition that it do not touch upon the
independence of other provinces of the Empire, and
so interfere with the grant of self-government to the
other provinces.*

It is against the equity no less than the interests
of the Empire as a whole that any one band of
Englishmen should impede the industrial progress of
any other band.   It is by the crediting aid and
material support of the rest of the Empire that our
Colonies spring into being and continue to rise in
stable prosperity.   England sent money, brains, skill,
and muscle to Victoria, as she is now sending them
to Natal.   So is a prosperous community originated.
Is that community to turn round and, with scant
thanks, say, ' Now you have given us all we require,
we will, if you please, keep all this for ourselves, and
not allow the rest of the Empire to participate in the
benefits it has conferred on us ' ? Communities of Englishmen, at all events, are not likely to proceed on
these pleas. They may, for the nonce, be led astray to
consider they are doing themselves good by protection or other such policy, but they will recognise, at
the same time, that not only their duty but also
their interest lies in maintaining the spirit and the
principles that have brought their race all its signal
prosperity.   It may be held, then, that with all the

various grades of self-governing communities which form the British nation at the present time, some means of expression is surely attainable which shall make all acknowledge *in their various degrees of constitutional spontaneity* the essential utility and so the absolutely binding nature of freedom of exchange within the boundaries of the Empire.

The St. Stephen's Parliament takes direct fiscal charge of most of our Colonies. Many of these have been with extraordinary success made into absolutely free ports. Such are the thriving entrepôts of commerce, Hong Kong, Singapore, and Gibraltar. There remain those groups of Colonies possessing the right of spontaneous action in this matter — in Canada, in Australia, and in South Africa.

These three cases differ essentially from one another. In Canada we have a community of some four millions in political contiguity to an energetic foreign state of some fifty millions. This state, keeping closed its own markets against Canadian produce, attempted to flood Canadian markets. The Canadians, in natural pique, raised up the wall of a high tariff to stay this evil. This policy has been inspired by two motives, the one to force the United States to a policy of reciprocity at all events, if not of mutual free trade ; the other simply to reserve

M 2

the Canadian market at all events for Canadian produce. This latter is no doubt the policy most in
favour with Canadians. They feel there is dangerous
similarity between the products of Canada and of
the States, these being the resultants of similar
natural and human forces. They know the competition of the larger threatens to swamp that of the
smaller. Canada feels that if she be shut out from
her own market her case is hopeless. And yet the
case is little mended by her shutting herself up in
her own market. Happily for Canada she yet
retains, if she will, the market of the world through
England. England is eager to buy of Canada if
Canada will only buy of England ; and in this case
there is no destructive competition because the products exchanged are the resultants of very diverse
natural and human forces. Such a policy at once
opens up the whole world as a market for Canadian
produce. It enables Canada to compete, at insuperable advantage, with the United States for English custom. Englishmen will naturally purchase
American produce *where* they can pay for it
'in kind.' Trade always flows in those channels
where it meets with least obstruction. The ship
that leaves England to load with wheat will
always go by preference to that port where an

outward cargo of English products can be sold with least obstruction.

The case of the Australians is of a totally different character. Here we have seven large Colonies at the present existing in total fiscal independence of one another. But as these seven Colonies fill up with population they feel more and more their geographical contiguity ; and already in addition to the increasing expense of collection of duties along thousands of miles of border, all the evils incident to fettered intercourse are rapidly developing. At the recent conference in Sydney every Colony, with the single exception of Victoria, strongly supported a movement in favour of a uniform and *low* tariff for all the Australasian Colonies.

And Australians are looking further afield. They know that each one's staple products—wool, and wine, and gold, and wheat, and meat—are exactly similar; the resultants of precisely similar natural and human forces. Thus, if they would achieve a right prosperity, they must exchange them with other commodities, the resultants of differing natural and human forces. This is necessary if they would secure the rewards due to their peculiar productions. Australians, both before and after the question of a customs union amongst themselves, will be ready to acknowledge the high benefits of assured freedom of exchange in the widespreading and varied market of the British Empire.

The case of South Africa just now occupies prominent public attention   The quarter-million of Europeans colonising South Africa have been and are unable to hold their own physically with the vast hordes of natives within and without the territory they have taken on themselves to civilize.   The rest of the Empire aids them in this their uphill task. Were it not for this aid, the European element in South Africa would long ago have been driven into the sea.   The people of England are paying to retain South Africa as a market for their wares and as an area of supply.   They have the right, let us hope they will have the reason, to see to it that they are repaid by the mutual benefits of freedom of commercial intercourse.   The Cape Colony, alone in South Africa, has fiscal independence of the Home Government.   But the Cape is as much interested as any to secure permanent European supremacy over the African natives.   This can only be secured by the permanence of English aid, and the price of this, a price the wise men at the Cape will, for their own interest, willingly pay, is the secured assurance of freedom of exchange with the rest of the Empire.

All the Colonies *must* feel that commercial union is even more important for them than for England. They know they obtain, by means of continued connection with England, safety and credit; those two pillars of prosperity which alone support a community from sinking under hostile aggression or commercial restriction. But *this connection is a tie which must depend in the main on identity of material interests.* And this identity can only be preserved by the means of commercial union.

All these Colonies *do* feel that commercial union is desirable. Indeed we have just witnessed in England what may be described as the first combined act of our Colonies on approaching manhood; the first great move in Imperial politics that has originated in the Colonies. Accredited representatives of their interests have met in London, and with the assistance of leading Englishmen have founded an association " for the promotion of the commercial interests of the British Empire, and for the preservation of its unity and integrity to draw closer the trade relations between its various component territories." This is a startling reply to those who in ignorance conceived that the colonists, the very men who, by the indubitable standard of practical success, were admittedly the best judges, made no move in the matter. *That the Colonists should come to England and agitate in favour of low tariffs throughout the Empire is a most welcome sign of the increased vitality of the English race.* It remains for those to whom the prosperity of their nation is matter of concern to support and recognise this wholesome movement.

§ 5. The British Constitution has, then, to be drawn upon to provide for a new development which has grown up with the growth of the Empire, and which presses on us as the inseparable accompaniment of the continued prosperity of the Empire. It needs no keen sight to see that community of material interests is crying aloud for unfettered commercial intercourse; and we know that community of national sentiment and tradition, as well as of enterprise and industry, yet flourishes in the nation; and that this community is the one powerful agent in any national effort. We have a national consciousness of the right end : statesmanship has to see that efficient means are adopted to give effect to this consciousness.

I must own that the one main fact graven on my own mind after sojourning in nearly every one of our Colonies is the fact that the English nation, *if it remains in close commercial union,* is only in the infancy of its career. All great statesmen who have understood our Colonies have come to this conclusion. Earl Russell summarised the case in the strong words, "There is no greater benefit to mankind that a statesman can propose to himself than the consolidation of the British Empire."

And great statesmen have discussed the means to this end. Lord Grey, in an article in the *Nineteenth Century*, has shown most amply and conclusively the great material injury that attempts at Protection in our Colonies have done to their own individual prosperity as well as to the commerce and industries of Great Britain. He laments with great power of reason the policy that has prevailed in late years of relinquishing the control previously exerted by the Imperial Parliament over the commercial policies of our Colonies ; and he would resuscitate the ancient ' Committee of Council for Trade and Plantations ; ' and, with the aid of the various Agents-General of our self-governing Colonies, *set up in England a body of such authority and influence as to justify Imperial supervision of all Colonial commercial policy in the spirit of justice to all members of the Empire.*

It may not be without advantage to set side by side with this yet another scheme with similar aim. The essential principle of procedure is simple. The

Imperial Parliament resumes its supreme control
over the commercial as distinct from the fiscal
policies of the Empire; but in so doing it takes
ample cognisance of the fact that large portions of
the Empire have a prescriptive constitutional voice
in this rearrangement. Indeed, action should be
taken on the invitation of the various self-governing Colonies. There must be combination and
mutual agreement, quasi-diplomatic if necessary, in
favour of low tariffs throughout the Empire. And
the Imperial Parliament will be charged with the
task of defending and maintaining for the future
this new charter of industrial prosperity. It is true
the United States will not allow local tariffs even for
the purpose of raising revenue; but the low tariff
necessary for revenue purposes is practically but little
hindrance to trade. All that is necessary is that, by
the direct means of the spontaneous action of enlight-
ened local government, and by the indirect influence
of advice and information, *the various communities of
the British Empire may come to subscribe, each in its
own degree of autonomous action, to an agreement to
keep its tariffs low.* For this purpose one of two principles would suffice. Earl Russell suggested the one,
viz., that no customs duties should exceed a certain
ad valorem percentage. A second principle would be

the rule that no customs duty be levied for any purpose save that of raising revenue. Thus could be
secured the inauguration of that free exchange of
products between all Englishmen which, if we regard
the teachings of the past, augurs a future of unprecedented prosperity.

§ 6. I have reserved till the last what is perhaps
the most important point in the whole case; and
that is the question as to the position such a commercially unified Empire is to hold to outsiders.
The courses possible are practically reduced to two
—the one the exclusion of outsiders, the other the
non-exclusion of outsiders.

To exclude outsiders is to appeal to the selfish
concurrence of one or two interests affected favourably by such action. It is not and cannot be denied
that the nation as a whole must be the loser. All
see there is no reason in a policy which shuts off
supplies and custom other communities are willing
to afford. The advocates of this policy have but one
plea that is likely to obtain patient hearing. This is
the plea that high duties to those outside the union
are the sole means to inducing those outsiders to
lower their tariffs and join the union.

It is even said that without some such national
fence Colonies themselves will be loth to join. I

have already given the grand answer to this contention in noting the recent actions and expressions
proceeding from the Colonies themselves. This point
is sometimes not quite grasped in high places; the
feelings and acts of two only of our forty Colonies,
because they chance to be feelings and acts that run
counter to the general national tendencies, are apt
to assume undue prominence, and have even been
regarded as typical of the acts and feelings of the
whole. They are distinctly not so. All the encouragement our Colonies require is the guarantee
that low tariffs shall exist *en permanence* in *all*
British markets.

The alternative plan, the non-exclusion of outsiders, implies a low tariff for all without exception.
It is a plan which will ultimately prevail if only we
pay any heed whatever to reason, experience, and
expediency. A low tariff all over this vast agglomeration of English markets will supply all these
markets with products at their lowest cost of production. Each English community will then batten
on the fact, which has done so much to enrich
England, that whatever it uses or consumes will be
obtained at the lowest cost possible. This is the
one main condition of profitable production. This
plan prevents any portion of the nation wasting its

energies on products that can be produced cheaper elsewhere.

For instance, for many years to come the Colonies, if they judge aright of their real economic position, will be the natural markets for manufactures, the natural producers of raw materials. Manufactories only thrive in centres of dense population. Sparse populations, occupying vast tracts of fertile and virgin soil, if they would profit most will produce cotton, and wool, and wheat, and minerals. Among such populations, if there is no baneful interference of high tariffs to subvert the natural order of prosperity, our home manufacturers will be assured natural and extensive markets for their wares, and reliable and inexhaustible supplies of those raw materials and food-stuffs which we are prevented producing in these islands by reason of the fact that our manufactures employ a population too dense for so utilising our limited area of soil. We have to live on and not out of our soil, because we are in the manufacturing and not the pastoral or agricultural stage. Our Colonies are in these other stages, and *to keep tariffs low is to enable all to profit by one another's opportunities through the medium of free exchange.*

That a high tariff for outsiders is unnecessary, we

see when we remember the natural expediency of a
low tariff. Trade is forced, by the insuperable power
of its own inherent attributes, to flow along that
channel which has fewest obstructions. Interchange
of products always does and always will thrive and
increase most where there are fewest restrictions.
To that community, in which low tariffs are established with certainty of no upward change, trade
will be diverted by the damning obstructions of
high tariffs elsewhere. In this we shall find the
natural 'sanction' that low tariffs, permanently
established over the British Empire, will increase
the interchange of products, and in so far develop
every industry and enterprise.

There will be a natural tendency to buy our
wheat of Canada and not of the States when we
know our manufacturers meet with no obstruction
in the one case, and with every obstruction in the
other. And we shall take not only wheat but
watches, or lard, or any other specialty of American
production for which Canadian soil or people may
develop special aptitude. And so with Australia,
or India, or the Cape, we shall go to them naturally
for our wool and our tea and our wine, if outward
cargoes of manufactures can be sent in the ships
that fetch home these goods.

With low tariffs so established over the British Empire we shall win the vast advantage of being less affected by the actions of foreign and independent countries. These actions, by the reason of their uncertainty, have been our bane in the past, and bid fair to be our bane in the future. We made treaties to obtain for ourselves wider markets and wider areas of supplies in the days when we had only foreign countries open to us. But now our own kith and kin, we ourselves, have become possessed of countries offering in the future more than the equivalent of these markets and these areas; and by the simple expedient of preventing the rise of restrictions on commercial intercourse we are likely to secure these markets and these areas, and to win for ourselves exemption from the only compelling power that of old forced us to seek to conciliate foreign powers. We can now, if we will, take our stand on our own self-sufficing independence. On this secure ground we can tell foreign nations we have no need of treaties. We are our own market and our own source of supply; and if foreign nations bar themselves by high tariffs from the great benefits of free intercourse, it concerns them indeed, but it concerns us no longer. The new British Empire affords us other avenues and other openings.

The malign influence of differential duties, elaborate treaties, bounties, reciprocity, retaliation, and even protection itself, together with all the evils incident to the interference of policies having no political, national, or economic connection with countries they deleteriously affect, will all be banished from within the frontiers of the British Empire. Their evil results will recoil on the foreigners alone, and leave the reproductive energy of our vast Empire to work out its own great prosperity untrammelled and unimpeded; with that true freedom of action which consists in the power of acting independently of foreign determining causes, and which is the condition most essential to the success of that human co-operation or 'bandwork' which has been shown to be the one main lever of human prosperity.

CHAPTER VIII.

FOREIGN COMPETITION IN AGRICULTURE.

§ 1. The British Islands are becoming more Manufacturing and well-to-do, and less purely Agricultural. § 2. American Prairie-cropping must in a few years wear itself out. § 3. The price of American Wheat must increase. § 4. America becomes rapidly populated. § 5. Americans really compete chiefly with our other Foreign Purveyors. § 6. Canada will supply Wheat, but not at permanently lower prices. § 7. English Wheat-growing has many intrinsic and local advantages. § 8. Foreign Competition has roused English Agriculture to improve itself.

§ 1. NOT long ago it was held that Agriculture was by far the largest of English industries. And although, since these good old days, we have become more than ever a nation of shopkeepers, and carriers, and manufacturers, we nevertheless continue to farm, and to farm well, as much land in these islands as we can obtain for the purpose. It may be true nowadays that but a portion of the

N

population is really connected with the land, so far as the earning its livelihood is concerned. But then the *whole* of the rest of the population lives by eating the produce of the soil; and so, after all, the utilisation of its soil is, to Britain as to every other nation, a primary concern. It is no wonder, then, that our agricultural prosperity or depression affects every fraction of the community, and that the recent bad seasons have stirred up a widespread public agitation on the subject of land generally.

Pending the results of the labours of the Royal Agricultural Commission, much good and useful work has been done towards creating a correct public opinion in this matter; and yet, if we may judge by their utterances, both public and private, it is only too common to find a most gloomy view of things which materially affects their energies and their enterprise, taken by the two classes more directly concerned—the great farming class on the one hand, and, on the other, that large proportion of wage-earners in this industry, whose winnings only too frequently barely cover the expenses of subsistence. To dispel this unnecessary but not unnatural gloom there is only needed the light of a wider knowledge of facts; and a more thoughtful heed to the actual conditions, past, future, and present.

This atmosphere of gloom is greatly brightened if we pay even momentary attention to the history of the past twenty years. Hereby we immediately recognise the radical modifications that have been imposed on English agriculture by increase of population *plus* increase of wealth. These two must be taken together. Even in the last ten years, while population has been found at the Census of 1881 to have increased about 11 per cent., wealth has increased 30 per cent. Trade, commerce, manufactures, and facilities of communication have all increased with even greater speed. This is no mere increase of mass of human beings, but of spending, and, above all, of working human beings. The British hive has not only increased in numbers, but both the reason and the result of this increase in numbers is increased production of wealth. The population is not only larger, it is also more busy and more well-to-do.

The direct effects of this growth on agriculture are twofold:—on the one hand we have a new use for large areas of soil; on the other hand we have greatly increased means for the purchase of food grown elsewhere. We have manufactories, railways, canals,

N 2

docks, mines, and so forth, ousting agriculture from areas of soil that in the aggregate sum up an important total. We have cities, towns, far-reaching suburbs, garden-surrounded villas, and great parks rapidly extending themselves over the land. And *these carry in their hands the proof of their utility in the higher price by which they buy out agriculture from its occupation of the soil.* The nation has so developed that it becomes more profitable to utilise the soil for these productive or residential purposes than for the growth of food alone. It will be found on calculation that the land so occupied is a no inconsiderable portion of the total area in our islands that can produce food. But this new occupation is a type or sign of what is going forward among us.

Another sign of progress is the fact that annually we import as much wheat as we grow, simply that the population may be fed. The signal importance of this fact will be appreciated by farmers when they bear in mind its necessary corollary, that if we would feed Englishmen on home-grown bread and no other we must actually double the acreage devoted to wheat-growing. On this analogy, in regard to the food-supply generally, we must double the area we farm. *But* we already farm 50 of the 80 millions of acres, which is all the sea allows these islands to possess. It is then a physical impossibility to double the area, and to double the whole production is certainly beyond the dreams of the most extravagant of 'scientific farmers,' considering the fact that, acre for acre cultivated for the purpose, English farmers already produce far more than farmers of any other nation. We may, as knowledge advances, increase our total produced; we cannot do so to any large extent; nor can we extend the productive area to any large extent. We must be content, as a prosperous, industrial nation, to buy much of our food elsewhere.

That the nation accepts and makes the most of these incidents of its growth is seen in the fact that of the food we import one-third at the least is food of a kind euphemistically described in the returns as that 'not usually produced' in the British Islands. We are not only importing food, but we are enjoying, in addition, that variety and plenty which results from our ability to lay under contribution the uttermost ends of the earth. Iceland moss and Ascension turtles, Canadian apples and Guinea cocoa-nuts, Australian meat and Californian barley, assure for the English market not only variety but certainty of supply.

Thus, while the producer has continued to produce as of old, the consumer has asserted the natural order of things, and sought abroad for the supplies necessitated by the great increase in demand. New developments in industry and commerce supply the wherewithal for the purchase of this extra food. And if we thus give proper prominence to the immediate past, and recognise the true nature of the national growth, we see that foreign supplies of food are a necessity of our new position, and that 'foreign competition' in this supply' is in very great measure no competition at all, but merely the supply in quantity, no less than in kind, of food that the physical limits of British agriculture forbid the English farmer to supply.

§ 2. But this appearance of the foreigner in the English food market has created a kind of panic, and for the nonce the British agricultural brain appears to be bereft of its accustomed shrewdness. Among the more important foundations of a sound judgment of the present, is a proper estimate of the probabilities of the near future. This is an estimate which has been strangely ignored. Unkindly seasons and low prices seem to have riveted attention on the gloomy present, and the eye of intelligence is thereby prevented from looking into the past for the sure and only prognostics of the future. For instance, 'American competition' is a bugbear only if we disregard the future as well as the past of the United States. Prairie-farming for the supply of the home and the European market is an industry of recent growth and developed under most peculiar conditions. Meat and wheat are produced on the spot at low prices. In twenty or thirty years' time at the most this industry will be at an end, so far as the maintenance of the present prices is concerned.

The United States at the present is an under-peopled but fertile country. At present there are vast tracts of virgin soil awaiting development. With Nature so favourable to its advances, a large community, with every appliance of an eminently practical civilization at its command, has but little difficulty in at once and with ease procuring a lavish supply of foods. But in such cases there exists a tendency—and the United States are no exception to the rule—for this very facility of production to outrun prudential methods of production. Wheat-growing in the United States has afforded a notable example of this tendency. The more settled and populated districts on the east coast had developed a system of farming but little differing from that

prevailing in the fully-peopled communities of the
European continent. But, as the increasing population pushed westwards, vast tracts of wheat-
producing soil were opened up by energetic men
greedy of present results. Wheat became, to adopt
Sir T. Brassey's happy phrase, 'the ready-money crop
of the pioneer farmer.' But the system of cultivation adopted was the 'earth-scratching' of Gibbon
Wakefield; and the profits of the system hung
on the very roughest cultivation and the very
cheapest access to the soil.

But even so, this rough prairie-cropping was soon
found to be liable to unexpected risks. Success in
the 'Far West' was frequently checked by causes
to which the English farmer is happily a stranger.
The farms are necessarily extensive; and, with this
cropping on a vast scale, weeds, as if inspired by
the surroundings, appear in quantities commensurate
with the true magnitude of American operations,
and on a scale inconceivable in carefully cultivated
England. Weeds have been known so to choke
a whole crop as to render it absolutely not worth
the ingathering. And there are plains in California
State, all part and parcel of the boasted 'wheat
area,' which enjoy a rainfall sufficient for a crop
only once in four or five years. And there are

seasons when all the scanty crops are consumed by
locusts and grasshoppers. Again, the danger of
prairie fires is greater the greater the area covered
by wheat.

These and other risks are further supplemented
by the fact that the supply of labour in these
wilder States is not only precarious, but is very
frequently absent at the critical times. A new
mining rush, busy times reviving suddenly in other
districts, or other counter-attractions, not infrequently force the farmer to leave good crops to rot
where they stand from the sheer absence of the
physical labour necessary for the harvesting. And
there are other surroundings of this prairie-farming
that do not readily occur to the English mind.
Thus, for instance, it is found that for every four
acres devoted to wheat one acre has to be cropped
in fodder for the support of the horses or cattle
necessary for carrying on the farming operations.
Or, again, grain has been often known to ripen too
quickly and to turn out ruinously light in the ear.

These are among the drags peculiar to the rough
cropping of the prairie. But, by way of antidote to
these, we find access to the soil is remarkably
cheap; labour is only needed in small quantities;
machinery can, in great measure, be made its

substitute; and little more capital is invested or *risked* than suffices to pay for sufficient seed. Thus in lucky seasons the price of wheat on the spot is proportionately low under present conditions.

§ 3. But it is important to remember that the price of this wheat on the spot and its price in England are two totally distinct facts. And, again, the price in England now and the price in England hereafter are no less distinct. And, after all, this price is the main item for the British farmer. It is well, then, to note the facts and prospects of the several elements of this price of American wheat in the English market; among these we find cost of production on the spot, cost of carriage, influence of middlemen, and, lastly, the fact that numerous other countries supply our markets with wheat.

In regard to the first of these elements, the paradox may be advanced with truth that the cheaper wheat is produced in the prairie the sooner will it disappear from the English market. The low price on the spot prevailing at present depends on the abnormally cheap use of good virgin soil, and on the possibility of a system of cropping, (for it cannot properly be termed cultivation,) which obtains large present returns on insignificant outlay. This method necessitates a continual taking up of new land and a continued abandoning of that which has been cropped. And even in the United States there is a physical limit to virgin prairie-lands that will grow wheat. The saying is attributed to the eminent American economist, Carey, that by thus growing wheat for export, Americans were exporting their own soil. The truth of this saying may be seen in the impoverished tracts from which all the good has already been literally exported. The cheaper wheat can be produced by this system of cropping the more rapidly does this wave of exhausting energy pass over the land.

Several results follow. In the first place, so far as this pioneer wheat-growing and prairie-grazing succeeds (or, in other words, pays) in the same proportion does it attract people. For, as Adam Smith puts it, people congregate where they can live cheapest. This incidental increase of population on the spot, due to the lowness of cost of production, at once raises cost of production. The first pioneer takes up his 10,000 acres, and for his first year's crop he feeds his cattle and horses on hay, cut gratis on the surrounding prairie—but in a year or two these surrounding prairies are also taken up, and he is forced to devote 2,000 of his acres to growing fodder—he is deprived of so much of his ready-money crop. The price of the remainder must rise if he is to reap the same profits. And again, this cropping is the work of man, and this increase of population largely stimulates the consumption on the spot of food produced in the district for both man and beast. And again, the competition incident to this increase of population sends up the value of this access to the soil; cultivation has to succeed to cropping; the terms 'manure,' and 'drainage,' and 'water-supply' are introduced to common use; and the farming that ensues produces wheat but little cheaper than it is produced in more fully peopled lands.

In the second place, this cheap production of wheat on the prairie is a result which acts as a cause of the rapid increase of the population of the States. The United States in good years produce at the present 350 million bushels of wheat, which, at the English average of consumption, is sufficient for, say, 70 million people. This conclusion is verified by the fact that the United States, with a population of 50 millions, exports one-third of the wheat produced. But if we calculate on the average increase of the population of the United States for the past eighty years, we see that the number of the population twenty years hence will be 100 millions. In other words, by the close of this century there will be added to the population of the United States a mass of human beings consuming *three times the amount* of wheat the United States now export. If the European market is still to receive the amount of wheat that now comes to it from the United States, Americans will have to produce about double the amount of wheat they now produce ; and they will have to produce it at the same low price if English farmers are to be any way concerned.

But it may well be asked where in the United States are new fresh wheat-producing areas to be found sufficient for this gigantic purpose ? Even the short history of this prairie-farming incontestably proves that as this cropping-wave succeeds in overrunning new ground out West, it recedes, *pari passu,* from old ground, so far as this cheap method of cropping is concerned. In the doubling of the area at present in use we must allow for what is deserted in the process. For if we include the farming of the old ground we find at once increased cost of production.

But even if we grant the most extravagant anticipations of prairie-farmers, and agree that this

cheap production of wheat will still be possible, we
are faced by another fact of experience already
amply demonstrated. The cheaper the production
of wheat in the prairie, the less the production of
wheat in better-farmed districts *in America* itself.
The home market, rapidly increasing in its consumptive demands, rapidly loses its former sources
of supply. To feed itself only, the American nation,
by the end of this century, would have to nearly
double its present production of wheat. If this is
all to be accomplished by the prairie process, this
process will have to be *trebled* in effect by reason
of its incidental action in destroying other national
sources of supply. The very cheapness of this prairie
method, if continued, would cause it more and more
to confine its energies to the supply of the home
market. And this home market of the United
States is in its infancy, and it will be centuries
before even the 'magnificent resources' of this
large area can be so utilised as to outrun these
local demands in the supply of wheat.

But at the least as important an element in
this matter of price is the cost of carriage. There
is truth here, also, in a paradox. The cheaper the
cost of carriage in the present the sooner will it
rise to a height barring present prices. If freights

and rates had been at normal heights a long-continued and steady trade might have been possible; but freight and rates have been the resultant of altogether abnormal conditions; and their very lowness will largely stimulate and hasten the maturity of normal conditions altogether prohibitive of such facilities for export.

However true it may be that, at the present, in favourable years wheat and meat are produced on the spot at remarkably low prices, yet the market for such large supplies of food is a long way off, and the very industry itself would never have come into being but for the fortuitous co-existence of altogether abnormal facilities of carriage. The people of the United States early determined to spread over their vast territories an elaborately planned network of waterways and railways. Means of communication were not only devised but perfected long before the necessities of communication had grown up. This proleptic action owed the fact of its realization to the abundance of capital, chiefly in other lands, that chanced at the moment to be anxiously looking for employment. But the railways were before their time; no dividends were forthcoming; and they passed, for the most part, into the hands of mortgagees. Much of their first

cost was dropped in the operation. The immediate
future seeks only to provide interest on this diminished capital. Thus, for the present, over such
portions as are now completed it positively pays
to carry goods at rates a few years ago deemed
inconceivable, and which, not many years hence,
will be altogether impossible.

The very lowness of these rates was thus the
opportunity of prairie-farming. Thus is supplied
the incentive and, in addition, the means to populating large areas. The march of the invading
immigrants has already reached far into these
wheat-producing districts. Towns, or rather cities,
have sprung up with the proverbial American
rapidity. Thus the very lowness of rates will
hasten the development of the social conditions
for which the railways have been planned and
constructed. But this pioneer wheat-growing has
been more than mere result, it has also been cause
of more vigorous extension of railways. It has
afforded forcible pretext for the present and hasty
realization of plans schemed for more populated
times. And even the very abandonment of cropped
for virgin areas has further stimulated this movement. Competition among the railways, with a
view to securing future benefits, the excuse of

promoters that their schemes must be realized in full before they can pay, the forced interposition of the mortgagees, and other causes, intrinsic and extrinsic, have enabled American railways in recent years to lower their rates beyond all belief. These causes are temporary, and contingent upon the peopling up of the country. There are powerful groups watching for their long-deferred profits. The finance of American railways is now chiefly in the hands of such groups. It stands to reason that if wheat can now be thrown upon the European market shillings per quarter below average prices, these railway financiers, if they retain any spark of the astuteness for which they have been famed in the past, will of a certainty judiciously tap this new source of revenue. In due measure will this action raise again the price of American wheat in foreign markets. It will be the object of these financiers to maintain the price of wheat at the highest rate commensurate with the continuance of the trade. The details of sharing the new profits will have to be arranged between the farmer and the companies, but the price will and must be enhanced in the operation.

But even this arrangement as to price is subject to another important factor, viz., the influence

of the indispensable middleman. A commodity
in general demand, and produced in such vast
quantities and in large proportion for distant
markets, must necessarily pass through the hands
of middlemen. The prices must be regulated in
accordance with what are or may be the needs of
distant communities. The prescience on which
these middlemen must needs depend is often at
fault : now it is too daring, now insufficiently so.
This raises the ultimate price of the commodity
dealt with. It thus comes to pass that wheat has
actually been purchased in Liverpool for less than
was paid for it in Chicago. And, on the other
hand, large fortunes have been made out of wheat
by buying it in Chicago and selling it within the
month in Liverpool. The recent gigantic specula-
tion known as the ' Keene wheat corner ' is typical
of these things. The partners in this ' pool ' held
at one time as much as sixteen million bushels
of wheat, and thus obtained complete command of
the market for the sake of their own advancement.

§ 4. The last element of this important feature
of price to which we need revert is the fact that the
English market numbers among its purveyors others
besides Americans. We in England have for years

past imported wheat on an annual average sufficient to feed fifteen millions of people. Last year, because of short harvests, we imported. sufficient for twenty millions. The United States, in *good years*, produce an exportable surplus sufficient to feed twenty millions of people; but a large proportion of this does not reach the English market. The great sting of this American competition will be felt by our foreign purveyors, more especially in all such years as we ourselves are blessed with good harvests.

I have adverted to the fact that this prairie-farming has already scotched one source whence supplies would have reached the English market. The New York and New England farmers have been forced to cease competing with the wheat supplies from the West. Prairie-farming has thus created for itself a great gap in the supply of the American home market, and in so far has diverted from export a large amount of its own produce.

But it is further necessary to remember that, although under these present exceptionally favourable conditions the United States grow one quarter the wheat the Western World consumes, yet not more than one quarter of what they grow is exported. The price of the wheat thus exported must become regulated by the prices prevailing in the

European markets. The United States supply to
Europe one-twelfth only of the annual supply. The
price of this twelfth must assimilate to that of the
remaining eleven-twelfths. The only imaginable obstacle in the way of this assimilation of prices is the
resolution of Americans, once they are established
in the European market, to refuse to take as much
as they can get for their commodity. The history
of American enterprise does not warrant such
expectations. The English farmer must remember
that American competition affects *all* the purveyors
of the English market, and not only of that, but of
the whole European market; and that, in this
larger view of the actual facts of the case; it will
at once be seen that even the low prices possible to
the present system of prairie-farming have a merely
fractional effect on the European market. What
then becomes of the claims put forward by
enthusiastic Western farmers to the effect that
their prairies are to become the granaries of the
world, and their capital the flour metropolis of
humanity? These sanguine anticipations, in the
ratio of their successful realization, would drive
wheat-cultivation out of Europe. The monopoly of
supply, and so of price, would fall to Americans.
But we must remember that the very existence of

the industry, and so of the monopoly, depends altogether on the continuance of those low prices which enabled it to come into existence. In a word, if these sanguine anticipations are to be realized Americans must accomplish the dual feat of quadrupling their present produce of wheat, and at the same time of maintaining the population of their country at the exact figure at which it stands at present. If they fail in either task the price of wheat must rise; and this rise would be the signal for the re-appearance of wheat-growing in Europe, and of the consequent fall of their monopoly.

The conditions I have now detailed combine to render possible for the present this large export of breadstuffs and food. The main fact for English farmers and landowners is that this *export* is from a fund on which Americans will not be able to draw much longer. Even under the present most favourable conditions of access to pasture and of freights, sound meat cannot always be placed in the English market below the price of *better* grown English meat. And similar conditions will soon arise in the supply of wheat. Thus a careful survey of the facts of the case brings us to the conclusion that, if present conditions continue, the great areas in the Western States will in, say ten years' time, be no longer able to export wheat and meat at prices below those which yield profit to the English farmer. In ten years' time 'American competition' in the English market will be in rapid natural decline. Thus the future of agriculture in the United States need not clash with the future of agriculture in the United Kingdom. And, after all, the prospects of English farming are in the future and not in the past, or even the present.

§ 5. In dealing with the competition in English markets of the United States, it is essential to a right judgment of this question to remember that Canada, in opening up her North-Western territories, has without doubt brought before the world a wheat-producing area of enormous extent. The soil and climate of that portion of this area already opened up produce crops double as heavy as those of the prairie lands in the States; and there are districts where continuous cropping for fifteen or even twenty years does not appear to exhaust the rich soil. Moreover the coming Canadian Pacific Railway is penetrating this area. It is not surprising, then, that with all these inspiriting prospects the sanguine pioneer farmers of the North-West should declare and, in a measure, prove their ability to produce and place wheat in the English market at an average little over 38*s.* a quarter.

But these sanguine anticipations must be taken *cum grano.* They are the first reports from a raw and untried district. And, indeed, the more we inquire into detail the more we find cause largely to discount these alleged anticipations. In the very first place we find the area has been gravely exaggerated, so far as wheat-production is concerned. Geographically, it may be true there are some 150 million acres awaiting the plough and the seed of the farmer, but practically it seems certain that a vast proportion of these acres will continue to wait till the end of time. Large curtailments of this area must be made owing to physical causes. And even where the climate is favourable, large tracts are found on inspection to be too sandy or too swampy for wheat, while in others there is dearth of water for the cattle that are indispensable in the carrying out of such extensive farming operations as are the main element in the cheap production of prairie wheat. Sinking wells, damming, draining, or irrigation—like manuring—are not adjuncts of prairie-farming, pure and simple. They add largely to the cost of production.

Again, although the crops are heavier than those

farther south, they are, nevertheless, found to be even more liable to the various scourges I have detailed. Fire has already eaten up valuable crops, and fire comes when all things are dry, in the autumn, when the crop is just ripe; grasshoppers and caterpillars have devastated large areas; the sun has been too favourable and ripened the ears too quickly for weight; and already the proof of these things is seen in that farmers, even in this much vaunted North-West, have been forced to sell out or to carry on at a loss through *bad* seasons and low prices.

A great point is the enormous interest (15 or 20 per cent.) now actually paid for money advanced for agricultural purposes on the *security of these new lands.* This is sure evidence of the existence of a deep-seated conviction that land will rise in value, and that such a rise will take place is of course a mere truism in the face of the advent of population. There is ample precedent in the eastern provinces of the Dominion. There agricultural land, manifestly and avowedly inferior to that of the North-West, is now worth 8*l.* and 10*l.* an acre. Such a price, when it comes to prevail in the North-West, will at once raise the price *on the spot* of wheat from 3*s.* 6*d.* to 5*s.* the bushel. Such a rise will not, however, take place unless and until the North-West proves its claim to be the wheat ground of America. But rise in the price of soil must accompany any and every step in the successful realization of these vast wheat-growing anticipations.

In this great North-West, *if* you can get your land at first prices, *if* you have good years, and *if* freights remain low, then you can export at a low price. But already these conditions are changing; already there is a steady enduring flow of population to the North-West. The farmers in the older provinces are either, taking to stock-raising and dairy and fruit farming or selling out and going west to grow wheat. Immigrants from all parts of Europe are seeking this great wheat area; it is the paradise of that large class of farmers who start without any great extent of capital. The great evidence of the fact of this vast migration is that the men who are already there farming on the borders of this area and getting their twenty and even thirty bushels to the acre, sell *all* they grow as seed and as food for these immigrants. Human beings are coming down on the land like a swarm of locusts; they and their beasts devouring what is reaped; and big cities springing up rapidly in their track. Not till this area is peopled will it export to any great extent. But by that time land will be far dearer—it has already doubled in value—and cost of production on the spot will rise *pro ratâ*.

And yet, in spite of all this, for long years to come wheat grown in the North-West must be grown *there* cheaper than it can be in England. The English farmer will find comfort in this, for he must also acknowledge that this fact makes the Canadian North-West the natural granary not of Europe but of America. Prairie-farming in the United States, obtaining ten to fourteen bushels per acre, at once substituted itself for the wheat-growing of the old Eastern States as the principal source of supply to the American market. The new method was prosecuted with such impetus and success that it also maintained and, in a small measure, increased the ratio that the export of wheat bore to other exports. The bright prospects of this Western farming were, however, destined to be ruthlessly disturbed by the discovery that the prairies north of the Canadian boundary line not only produced wheat but produced double the quantity, acre for acre, with no additional expenses. The inevitable and natural consequence is now following. The North-West is succeeding to the West as the West succeeded to the East.

We see, then, that there will be but little export from

the Canadian North-West till that North-West is peopled. In the next place, when so peopled, the cost of production on the spot will have risen considerably; and, lastly, the wheat so grown for export will find its chief market in America and not in Europe.

It is thus evident, if we give proper prominence to the immediate past and duly weigh the probabilities of the near future, that 'American' and other competition in agricultural matters is a fluctuating factor; and that it will wax and wane in accord with the growths and developments of other communities.

§ 6. There remains the task of facing the present, which we thus clearly understand, and seeing what good and true use may be made of it.

The farmer in these islands will remember that his dread of American competition was chiefly bred of an untoward and rare succession of bad harvests. But he will find on his own farm many substantial crumbs of comfort. In this matter of wheat, for instance, the farmer does not live by the ears alone; for even in the very production of these ears he gains 2s. a bushel on the American in the value of straw. This is an important item in wheat-growing; and on the prairie the straw is not only of no use but wastes the certain amount of labour necessary to burn it as rubbish. The getting rid of manure on the richer prairies is likewise an actual additional expense to the farmer. Again, the fertility of some English districts, when properly farmed, is so great that it outbids all possible prairie competition. The yield per acre is above competition. Again, in most good districts English wheat is of higher intrinsic value (often 3s. and 4s. the quarter) than any that can be grown on the prairie system. Again, we have Mr. Prout's records of his experiment of 'continuous wheat-growing' to show that even in the exceptionally bad years through which we have recently passed such "scientific agriculture" continues to yield profits.

Free Trade and density of population also range themselves on the side of the British farmer. Forty years of English progress have made fewer· more important marks on the state of affairs than in regard to agricultural labour. This commodity has now become certain in its supply and, as times go, cheap. It is 15 per cent. cheaper than labour of similar type in America. The fact is that both the farmer and the labourers he employs are in capital position as consumers. When our short wheat crop last year forced us to import half as much again of wheat as usual, there was a fall rather than a rise in price of this first necessary of life. The commercial policy England has adopted has enlarged greatly the general wealth chiefly by the channel of easier consumption. Our farmers, deprived of profits, by the cruelty of the season, as producers, nevertheless found compensation and relief as consumers in the accommodation afforded by the wisdom of the national policy.

§ 7. But though the weight of this American competition is temporary, and aggravated by reason of bad seasons in England, it will nevertheless have an abiding effect which is altogether salutary. Agriculture is an industry which has a proverbial tendency to extreme conservatism. Its very success seems to engender a condition of bucolic contentment which is little in keeping with these times of 'Progress.' The British landowner no less than the British farmer in the future will have cause for deep gratitude to his Transatlantic rival for rousing him to a sense of the needs of the day. It is one of the great benefits conferred by Free Trade, that where it prevails no industry can fall behind the best knowledge of the day. The United States have taught Europe the great fact that even in the most trivial tasks, the brain can be made the most profitable ally of the hand. English agriculturists have never been

wanting in shrewdness or in energy; they have
occasionally lagged in knowledge; and even this
recent short scare has set them thoroughly to work
on the science of agriculture. But this science must
not be confined to the chemical cultivation of the
soil or to the mere physiological processes of organic
growth—wisely and well it will be extended to
embrace the economic and political as well as the
natural factors of agricultural success. Commercial
geography and statistical information will prove as
precious to the English farmer as local lore of husbandry. It will henceforth be recognised as more
useful to know that in a particular series of years
pasture or roots will pay better than cereals because
of the state of distant competing markets, than to
abide by some chemically perfect rotation of crops.
It may be that for the immediate present, wheat-
cultivation that is not of the highest order will be in
abeyance in England. A true science of agriculture
shows the political reasons for this temporary subversion of natural courses. But this same knowledge
will again forewarn farmers of the time when the
fuller growth of America will enable the revival of
wheat-growing even on the poorer soils where for the
time it had been given up.

We may trust this American competition scare

especially to influence landowners. The report of
the tenant farmers' delegates to the Canadian North-
West are full of allusions to the highly profitable
absence in Canada of the interference of "lawyer
factors." The facts of this competition may awaken
us to the removal of what is antiquated in our
present system of land tenure. Adam Smith's
vigorous, nay, pathetic, denunciation of entails and
other 'remnants of feudal anarchy' have hitherto
made little impression; but now, coupled with these
lessons from America, such reasonings are likely to
generate a new zest in the minds and work both of
owners and tenants, and thus considerably to
enhance the profits that have for years been
carelessly deemed sufficient for landed property.

§ 8. Profits also will come from the transference
of agricultural activity. The general tendency of
this transference may be described as towards meat-
growing, dairy-farming, poultry-breeding, and
market gardening—in the words of Professor Aldis
—towards "the growth of such products as, from
their nature, must be consumed comparatively near
to their point of origin." No doubt the British
farmer will seek for crops and produce that are not
readily transported, by reason of their perishable,
bulky, or fragile nature. He will. come to regard

the risks and costs of carriage as his natural 'protection.' And he will come to learn that in other ways, in the superior productive power of the English soil and climate, and of the English system *or skill* in farming, he yet retains, if we judge by results, a sure pre-eminence. And he, of all men, will acknowledge that, after all, whatever the theory, the cause or the reason—the proof of the pudding is in the eating.

As an instance, the English agriculturist will ask himself, "How is it I do not grow beet for sugar-making? I know there is just twice the amount of beetroot grown in Europe for this purpose that there was only ten years ago; I know that England uses just twice as much beet-sugar as she used even ten years ago; I know our English refiners buy *abroad* every year nearly 200,000 tons of raw beet-sugar; I know root-crops in England produce more, acre for acre, than they do abroad. And yet I don't grow beet; I grumble that no crops pay nowadays; I don't suppose more than that can be said of beet. Caird and Duncan and such other authorities tell me I have a capital climate for the purpose. Am I in the position of the Irish before they grew the national potato? Am I still under the Napoleonic spell? I know Bonaparte started beet-growing on the Continent as one of his many devices for destroying England's commercial greatness, by the ruin of her sugar colonies. Can't I have my revenge by taking this leaf out of his book ? " And he will find his consoling answer in a matter-of-fact conclusion that he cannot tell till he tries.

It has been my object to focus the attention of agriculturists on a wider appreciation of the facts of the past as well as of the present, in order that we may judge aright of the future. The question of its food-supply is to any nation its primary concern, and the utilisation of the soil is a main element in this question. It is often mistaken for the whole of the question. It is well to bear in mind that since the inauguration of free trade we have added eight millions to our population, and we have increased our imports of food (of kinds usually grown in England) by something like 80,000,000*l.* value in the year. It may be said, then, that these new eight millions of people spend 10*l.* each per annum to pay for foreign supplies which they fail to obtain from English sources. Thus, seeing that our system of agriculture is more productive than that of other countries, we are driven to acknowledge that at least a partial cause of this purchasing abroad of these foods is that

P

we do not farm sufficient soil to feed our own population.

Two questions remain: Is this owing to actual lack of land? do we practically make the best of all the soil we possess that is fit for the purpose? Or, on the other hand, assuming that soil exists sufficient for the purpose, is not much of this now utilised for industries or purposes that pay better than the direct production of food? This latter explanation is, at all events, supported by the fact that annually we increase our consumption of foods that cannot be grown in England. In 1840 we spent 9s. per head per annum on these foreign foods. In 1878 we spent 30s. per head. As compared with pre-free-trade days, we now buy three times the amount of currants, ten times the amount of oranges and lemons, four times the amount of tea, and so in all other details. Manufactures, mining, and carrying have progressed in proportion; but population has only increased by one-fifth. We are driven, then, to the conclusion that capital, labour, and probably large areas of actual soil, have been turned to other and more profitable uses than the direct production of food. The Census records are significant. In 1841 the rural population of England and Wales (the portion, that is, connected with the direct production of food) numbered 8,200,000 ; the town population (that portion not connected with the direct production of food) numbered 7,700,000. The country folk outnumbered the townsfolk ; those who produced food outnumbered those who only consumed. But in 1871, while the rural population only increased its numbers by some 2,000,000, the town populations had increased by no less than 5,000,000. In 1871 the tables were reversed ; the townsfolk largely outnumbered the country folk—those who produced food were largely outnumbered by those who only consumed it. The Census of 1881 proved that the urban population continues to increase nearly twice as fast as the rural. We have more people, we have more money, and we have found for certain areas of soil more profitable use than the manufacture of food. What wonder, then, that the national food market is supplied in some measure by foreigners ?

We have thus, in brief, the whole case of this foreign competition. British agriculture will derive invaluable benefit from these alleged inroads on its prosperity if, as seems probable, this competition of virgin soils directly or indirectly rouse English agriculture to a survey of the needs of the day. By the close of this century, twenty years hence, prairie produce will be more and more absorbed in its own home market; and even wheat-growing in England may again have reverted to its old courses. English agriculture will then be found, without doubt, to have passed through the fire of competition improved vastly in quality, purged and hardened for a long future of prosperous activity.

CHAPTER IX.

FOREIGN COMPETITION IN MANUFACTURES.

§ 1. What Foreigners are doing and what they are asserted to
be doing. § 2. The modern tendencies of Foreign Tariffs.
§ 3. Of Colonial Tariffs. § 4. Pauperising effects of High
Tariffs. § 5. Foreign Exporters of Manufactures.

§ 1. THERE is no field of human industry for
which the aid of the State is more often invoked
than for that of manufactures. To start non-existent
manufactures; to foster and cherish manufactures
that are hard pressed; to protect all classes of
manufactures against foreign oppression or aggression;—are held by many to be among the first
duties of a national government. Such is the end
put forward. And to attain this end means are
suggested in which assumption and assertion entirely
swamp experience. Government are told to start
and cherish and protect manufactures by the means
and instrumentality of customs duties. What I
wish in this chapter to suggest is that these means

have proved by no means infallible. Indeed, if we
look to recorded results, we find that the lower the
customs tariff the more do manufactures originate,
progress, and prosper in a country. Experience tells
us that if you would start and encourage and maintain manufactures that shall be profitable to the
community, you must jealously watch that your
tariff of customs duties be low enough not to
interfere practically with the free course of industry.
There is no more self-evident proof of this to be
found anywhere than in the records of what manufacturers are actually doing in England and in
foreign countries. And these records belie in a
most astounding manner the assertions on the
subject that are, strange to say, commonplaces in
books and newspapers, no less than on the platform
and in the public utterances of those who aspire
to be leaders and advisers of the community at
large.

§ 2. One of the commonest of these assertions is
to the effect that "*Foreigners are by their tariffs
shutting us out of their markets,*" and that "*hostile
tariffs abroad are closing to our manufactures the
markets of the world.*" In the first place, this type
of assertion is absolutely and, in the second place,
it is relatively contradicted by the facts of the case.

It is absolutely untrue because, as a matter of fact, the various foreign countries have, for instance, during the last twenty years, in the aggregate taken great strides towards Free Trade principles in regulating their tariffs.

Lord Sandon did his party a sterling benefit by calling for a parliamentary return recording the rates of duty in English money levied on articles of British produce or manufacture imported into the various foreign countries and chief English Colonies in each of the years 1860, 1870, 1875, and 1880. These returns are now before the public, and to ignore them is to ignore recorded facts of the highest value at the present moment.

On the continent of Europe we find, from these returns, that during the last twenty years tariffs have been generally and considerably lowered; the numbers of articles taxed has been considerably reduced; and all the states of the Continent have either granted or expressed their willingness to grant most favoured nation treatment to English goods.

It may be well to place on record here a few of the details of this notable European movement.

In the first place, in regard to the tendency towards reduction of tariffs. Comparing the tariffs of 1880 with those of 1860, we find that in only two out of the sixteen European states is there any increase. These two exceptions are Italy and Greece. And even in these two cases there are explanations that are most satisfactory. In Italy the change is due to the fact that in 1880, by the lapse of special treaties between Italy and third countries, English imports fell under a 'general tariff' higher than that they had enjoyed under most favoured nation treatment. In Greece the change was due to the fact that all duties were raised 10 per cent. *ad valorem* by the promulgation of a financial law requiring all duties to be paid in new instead of old drachmas. Of the other states of Europe—in France and in Turkey the tariffs remained the same; in Denmark, Portugal, and Switzerland there has been reduction when there has been change; in Spain, Germany, Russia, Sweden, Norway, and Austria there has been general and, very often, great reduction.

A point of great additional importance is the number and kind of items in which alteration has been made. If we omit Italy and Greece on account of their present anomalous position, we find that of the 2,140 'items' existing in 1860, 136 only have been raised, while 900 have remained the same and no less than 1,104 have either been lowered or removed from the list altogether.

Or the 136 that have been raised, 30 are in Denmark, 53 in Germany and Russia, and the remaining 53 scattered over all other countries. It is desirable also to remember the kind of items so altered. In Denmark the increase has taken place in the duties on spirits, raw sugar, butter, and fire-arms. In Russia the increase has been in wool, engines, and machinery. In Germany the chief rise has been in yarns of various kinds. In Holland there has been increase on raw sugar. In Sweden and in Norway on spirits and raw sugar. In Austria on railway carriages. Generally speaking we find that the duties have been raised in 61 cases on yarns, raw materials, and food; in 20 on spirits; in 19 on tissues; and in 37 on sundry manufactured articles. Thus the English manufacturer has been directly favoured in many more instances than he has been directly hampered in the comparatively few instances in which duties have been raised on the Continent.

Incidentally it may be mentioned that in Russia alone a very great advance in favour of the English manufacturer has been made in the abolishing the distinction which was drawn in 1860 between goods arriving by sea and by land. Tissues, hosiery, carpets, earthenware, refined sugar, iron-castings, paper, and other items of English export, were all saddled with these extra duties in 1860 from which they were relieved in 1880.

As to the 1,104 items that have been lowered, the English exporter has even more definite cause to congratulate himself. In 200 cases there is a decrease in the duties levied on raw materials and food. In 400 cases there is a decrease in the duties on yarns and tissues, and the remaining 504 cases are in sundry items of manufactured articles.

Perhaps the most conclusive testimony is that which deals with the comparative height of the present tariffs. It may be held that a tariff not exceeding 10 per cent. *ad valorem* will not greatly interfere with trade. A tariff that is, in the aggregate average, above 20 per cent *ad valorem* may be set down as decidedly high and 'hostile.' An intermediate tariff may be described as medium. If, then, we classify continental countries under the three categories low, medium, and high, according as their tariffs are under 10 per cent., between 10 per cent. and 20 per cent., and above 20 per cent., we shall find that Switzerland, Turkey, Holland, Norway, Sweden, Belgium, and France, range themselves under the first category. Italy, Denmark, and Germany may be described as medium. Spain, Greece, Portugal, Austria, and Russia still remain under the category of high tariff countries. It is not our province to deal with prospects, but it may be mentioned that Italy, Portugal, and especially Spain, are determined to advance themselves out of this backward class so soon as they. can. It will thus be seen that during the last twenty years tariffs have been generally and considerably lowered on the continent of Europe.

We must also recognise the fact that the number of articles appearing in the tariffs has been very considerably reduced. In only three States — in Germany, Italy, and Denmark — has there been any increase in the number of items on the list. In the other States the average number of articles scheduled has fallen from 134 in 1860 to 118 in 1880. And there are now only three States that have more than 200 articles on their schedule. This tendency is of course a tendency invaluable to freedom of commerce, for it clears the channel of numerous obstructions that otherwise impede and hamper that free current of commercial intercourse which is so absolutely essential to a healthy state of trade.

Perhaps the most definite advance is, however,

the general adoption of the most favoured nation
principle. This is a great step out of the com-
plications and impediments to trade inevitable
to the system of many and separate commercial
treaties. It seems that in 1860 we enjoyed this
favour by express treaty with eight only of the
sixteen European states. In 1880 we had actually
secured the privilege with no less than fourteen,
and the remaining two had expressed their definite
determination to adopt the arrangement so soon
as treaties could be arranged. The high importance
of this increasing inclination of foreign nations to
give us most favoured nation treatment is seen in
the fact that it is one half the battle at the least in
our competition to supply a foreign market. We
have 'opposed' to us the native and the foreign
competitor; and this 'most favoured nation' treatment at once puts us on an equal footing with our
foreign competitor. As for the native competitor,
he, so far as he can compete at all, can only hope
to compete with success provided he enjoy the same
facilities as a consumer that we enjoy in consequence of low tariffs. We have thus advanced the
great step since 1860 which places us in nearly all
European markets on an equality with all foreign
competitors in those markets. This is a distinct

and general advance along the whole line in the
direction of greater freedom of commercial intercourse. And on the whole we see that on the
continent of Europe the tariffs are becoming less and
less hostile to English goods.

§ 3. A subsidiary but none the less common and
important complaint is put forward that *our Colonies
shut us out by hostile and Protective tariffs.* Indeed
Protectionists, not only in England but in other
countries, have twitted us with the assertion that
however 'Freetrade' we may be ourselves, nevertheless our colonial offspring, so soon as they acquire
fiscal liberty, immediately raise up hostile tariffs
against us, and adopt the policy of Protection for
themselves. This strange and utter misrepresenta-
tion of what is actually occurring holds sway over a
strangely wide domain. It is reflected in leading
articles in leading newspapers ; it is even a commonplace on the platform, in Parliament, and even
within the precincts of the Cobden Club itself.
Professor Bonamy Price is indeed one of the few
public authorities who has put the matter in its
true light. In an address in 1878 he well put
the matter in the sentence: "Victoria, at the
instigation of an ignorant democracy, breaks the
financial uniformity of a mighty empire, and loads

the merchandise of the central State with har-
rassing duties." As a matter of fact we have nine
Colonies that arrange their own fiscal affairs in
independence of the Colonial Office. Of these,
only two, Canada and Victoria, have 'hostile'
tariffs. The Cape of Good Hope, New South
Wales, Queensland, Tasmania, South Australia,
New Zealand, and Newfoundland, all have tariffs
that would fall under the 'low' category as being
under 10 per cent. They are all tariffs imposed
solely for the purposes of revenue. And of our
remaining Crown and other Colonies all have low
tariffs excepting, indeed, those which have no
tariffs at all.

Canada and Victoria have both of them set up
high tariffs within recent years for the special and
avowed purpose of Protection. But Victoria, as we
have seen in detail in a previous chapter, has
grievous cause to repent this fiscal backsliding. In
Canada the main reason for the adoption of a
Protective policy is political and not economical. It
is a measure of self-defence against the supposed
overshadowing of its great neighbour. The Canadian
Government determined to protect itself by a high
tariff against the United States. And, yielding only
to the definite law of the British Empire, that within

its boundaries there should be no differential duties, the high tariff had to include British as well as American goods though the Canadians themselves pointed out it was distinctly not hostile in intention to British goods.

Our Colonies and India are, as is very well known, taking from us vastly increasing quantities of manufactured commodities. As we see, they most of them have low tariffs; but it is a notable comment on the policy of high tariffs that the two Colonies that impose them still, continue to do their share in the consumption of manufactures from the mother country. The squatters and miners of Victoria no less than the farmers and lumberers of Canada are not to be turned aside from their most lucrative enterprises by any blandishments of Protection. The great bulk of population in each of these two Colonies sturdily refuses to reverse the natural and most profitable order of opening up a new country. All that the high tariff can do is to make these natural pioneers of their country's growth and greatness pay more for what they use. The high tariff is merely a tax on growth which is paid without difficulty out of the great profit that accrues from the rapid development of virgin resources. The amount of this tax may be fairly gauged in the comparison of Victoria and New South Wales we have made in a previous chapter.

§ 4. Recorded results tell us that the assertion that most other countries are exhibiting in their tariff arrangement increased hostility to British manufactures, is absolutely contrary to truth. The assertion is also relatively untrue. If we for one moment ask ourselves the question who pays import duties we shall at once see that a high tariff only excludes foreign goods in the sense of rendering the population of the protected country less able to buy these goods, whether of foreign or of home make. If it so happens that the country is rich in other wealth-yielding forces the general effect of the tariff will be, not to curtail the importation of foreign goods but, simply to force the population to pay more than other nations pay for these same goods. We still find that, in the strictly protected communities of the United States, Canada, and Victoria, the consumption of English manufactured articles, of the very kind the tariff seeks to exclude, nevertheless continues to increase year by year.

Supposing that a ton of linen piece-goods can be manufactured in England for 100*l.* Add to this 10*l.* profit and 1*l.* carriage to market. The English dealer can sell at a profit for 112*l.* The Germans place on this a duty of 5*l.* in order to protect their own linen industries. This difference is either pure profit to the German manufacturer or it represents extra cost of production. And so long as the higher price is paid by the German purchaser English goods may be able to compete, provided the added duty only brings up the total cost of the English goods to the level of the cost of production in Germany. In this sense the Import duty is merely the entrance-fee charged by the State for entry into the German market, which fee is recouped out of the higher prices obtaining in the market. And if these prices are not higher the protective tariff is of no effect.

The point of the question is, whether this entrance-fee can be recouped out of the differences of price. If it cannot, English goods will not penetrate ; but in that case the German State fails to obtain an equivalent amount for its Revenue ; and the German consumer has to contribute in some other way. But it all comes in the end to the issue that the amount of the Import duty that is paid is ultimately paid by the German consumer.

This tells terribly on production in Germany. The value of wages or of profits depends intimately on their purchasing power. If a Protective duty

Q

raises local prices 20 per cent. it makes labour 20 per
cent. dearer, and it makes profits 20 per cent. less
profitable. It is paid by the producers of the nation
quâ consumers. In the enhanced prices of his
clothing and his food the labourer will contribute
out of his wages. In the enhanced prices not only
of his clothing and food, but also of his machinery
and his raw materials, the capitalist will contribute
out of his profits.

If the duty succeeds in fostering, that is interfering with, industry, it can only do so by succeeding
in making the price of the commodity higher to the
consumer than it otherwise would be. And *pro tanto*
it reduces the earnings of labour and the profits of
capital. *Pro tanto* it is a dead loss to the producers ;
a dead handicap on the nation as a whole.

And there is further loss to the nation that
imposes import duties that are so high as to interfere with the free course of industry. We are
all struck by the fact that any nation famed for
wealth is a nation of great commercial dealings.
There is most capital made by those nations that
trade most. Exchange is the one great fountain
head of capital, whether it be local or cosmopolitan.
The reason is not commonly understood. The
popular mind with strange perversity vainly desires

that the nominal value of exports should balance
or exceed that of imports. The very reverse is, of
course, the more profitable account. It is out of
the profits made by importing that commerce en-
riches a nation. The exports are merely one of
many methods of paying for the imports. But
after they are paid for, imports bring with them
profit. We may put a hypothetical case. Very good
pine-apples can be grown in England at a cost of
2*s.* 6*d.* each: equally good pine-apples can be sent
from Jamaica at a cost of 6*d.* each, including 2*d.*
profit to the grower. Consequently we import
great quantities of pine-apples from Jamaica. Porter
cannot be made in Jamaica, so warm is the climate,
at less cost than 2*s.* 6*d.* a bottle. It can be made
in England at 6*d.* a bottle, including 2*d.* profit to
the brewer. The cost of carriage to and fro is
equal for a bottle or a pine-apple. We send to
Jamaica as exports 1,000 bottles of porter costing
25*l.* We receive from Jamaica 1,000 pine-apples
costing 25*l.* The brewer in England, by having a
market in Jamaica, has made 8*l.* profit; and so
too the pine-apple grower in Jamaica, by having a
market in England, has made 8*l.* profit. So far
each nation has been enriched. But there is a
far greater source of profit to each community in

the enormous saving of expense secured by the exchange. Supposing there to exist prohibitive tariffs in England against pine-apples and in Jamaica against porter. Then in one country, if they drank porter, consumers would have to pay 125*l.* instead of 25*l.* for the 1,000 bottles; and in the other country they would have to pay 125*l.* instead of 25*l.* for their 1,000 pine-apples. In other words, by the means of the protective tariff, Jamaica would have been impoverished 100*l.* and England 100*l.* in every such transaction.

It is in this respect that high and protective tariffs most injure English exporters. It is an indirect and not a direct effect. But it is none the less powerful and telling. A high tariff prevents a nation reaping all the profits which accrue from exchange; and the nation has so much the less to spend on the necessities, the conveniences, or the luxuries of life. In England, by our commerce, we can eat pine-apples for 6*d.* that would otherwise cost us 2*s.* 6*d.* And so, in proportion, with all other commodities, there is profit in whatever we consume or use by reason of our free imports. We leave trade unrestricted, and we know that then it will run in those channels and in those directions which are most favourable to the genesis of profits.

We regret to see other nations cutting themselves off from such sources of profit, and we are fain to console ourselves with the tendency there arises for us, profiting so as consumers, to cheapen so greatly our costs of production as to undermine altogether these walls that other nations build up in order to keep out the fertilising and enriching current of free commerce.

It is as though villages in the rainless Delta of the Nile were to fence themselves and their lands round with walls impermeable to the annual flooding of the Nile, and set to work to manufacture manures and distil water. Each year that river brings down, it is calculated, so many millions of tons of fertilising deposit and so many billions of gallons of water to a rainless land. Supposing that one of those villages adopts the opposite policy, and by clearing away all obstructions, invites and receives the full flood of the fertilising and enriching Nile; and supposing the remaining villages continue stoutly to keep out all such external aid—not only will this one village flourish, but its crops will become so perennially abundant that it will shortly find itself able to purchase with its surplus all that it desires of the property of its desolated neighbours.

And in the end, when, for lack of recuperative force; when, through despising the outside aid of more favoured regions of the earth; when, by reason of refusing to admit the waters of rainy and snowy Abyssinia, these villages of the rainless Delta dwindle and fall into ruin, then the wise village, which has made the most of the bounty of nature in other lands, will be flourishing as ever, and only regretting that the other villages should, by foolish exclusiveness, have so entirely pauperised themselves as to be no longer capable of purchasing its own surplus products.

So do nations, which open their doors to supplies from all the world, profit not only by the large and steady supply of all they need as consumers and as producers, but above all by the fact that wheresoever they can obtain a commodity abroad cheaper than it can be made at home—in every case there is enormous profit to the nation, simply out of the fact that it is not made at home at so much extra cost of national labour.

§ 5. It might be supposed, not altogether without reason, that, if our manufactures were in actual process of extinction by this asserted irruption of foreign competition, these various countries, and more especially those which foster their manufactures, would be all of them increasing the percentage of manufactures exported.

In his most admirable book *Freetrade v. Fairtrade,* Mr. T. H. Farrer gives the following tables, which tell no uncertain tale.

UNITED KINGDOM.

	1870.		1880.	
	Amount.	Per cent. of Total.	Amount.	Per cent. of Total.
	£		£	
Articles of Food, Drink, and Tobacco	7,607	4	8,825	4
Raw Materials	13,744	7	23,272	10
Manufactured Goods	178,236	89	190,963	86
Total Exports of British and Irish Produce .... }	199,587	100	223,060	100

UNITED STATES.

	AMOUNT.				PERCENTAGE.	
	1870.	1880.	1870	1880.	1870.	1880.
	Dollars.	Dollars.	* £	* £		
Food	129,960	464,130	21,660	96,694	28·6	56·3
Raw Materials .	273,597	274,554	45,600	57,199	60·1	33·3
Manufactured } Articles ... }	51,651	85,262	8,609	17,763	11·3	10·4
Total	455,208	823,946	75,869	171,656	100	100

FRANCE.

	AMOUNT.		PERCENTAGE.	
	1869.	1879.	1869.	1879.
	£	£		
Food.......................	34,017	33.159	27·0	26·0
Raw Materials	21,482	25,210	17·0	19·8
Manufactures...........................	70,504	69.516	56·0	54·2
Total	126,003	127,885	100	100

GERMANY.

	AMOUNT.				PERCENTAGE.	
	1869.	1879.	1869.	1879.	1869.	1879.
	Marks.	Marks.	£	£		
Food	567,126	758,970	28,356	37,948	25·6	27·3
Raw Materials.	767,660	945,660	38,383	47,283	34·7	34·0
Manufactured Articles ...	877,277	1,071,020	43,864	53,551	39·7	38·7
Total	2,212,063*	2,775,650	110,603*	138,782	100	100

* The values for 1869 are estimated only.

It will be observed that the percentage of manufactures to total exports decreases in proportion as
the tariff is higher and more avowedly protective.

It is well to compare particular points.

We are frequently warned that in textile manufactures our day of supremacy is past and gone.
And we are told France is wise in her generation

in keeping to an elaborate scale of duties. If we look to results we find that in supplying the markets of the world, we are not only at the present doing nearly five times the foreign business that France is doing, but within the last 20 years, while our export of textiles has *increased* 50 per cent. that of France has *decreased* 10 per cent. The figures are worthy of record :—

EXPORTS OF TEXTILE MANUFACTURES.
(Cotton, linen, silk, and woollen.)

	1859.	1869.	1879.	1880.
France	£32,000,000 ...	£35,000,000 ...	£28,000,000 ...	£29,000,000
England......	73,000,000 ...	107,000,000 ...	94,000,000 ...	109,000,000

Perhaps there is no State in the world that has set to work so determinedly to foster manufactures by the means of a high customs tariff as the United States. Mr. Mulhall in his valuable work *The Balance Sheet of Nations* gives some very remarkable figures. He tells us that in 1870 the inhabitants of these islands manufactured 408 shillings per head, but that in 1880 the value of the manufactures was 440 shillings per head—an increase of 8 per cent. In the same two years the value of manufactures per head of population in the United States was 354 and 355 shillings respectively. In other words, the population of the United Kingdom was becoming more and more a manufacturing people, while the population of the United States was remaining stationary in that very respect.

And it is not only with us that all this is so. The Swiss exports to the United States tell the same tale. There is increase in the watches exported, a very significant item.

Again—If we ask for the export of a manufactured commodity for which any country is famous, and if we also look to its tariff, we shall notice some curious facts. On the continent of Europe France is the great silk manufacturing country, Switzerland following next. In all European countries there are heavy import duties on silk, excepting only Switzerland, where there is a light duty, and France, where there is no duty at all.

Again fire-arms enter Belgium and Norway free, and all other continental States place import duties on them. Belgium, at all events, is the great continental manufactory of fire-arms, and the only one whose competition is actually felt by England.

Again it will be held that Switzerland is the head-quarters of European watch and clock making. And yet Switzerland of all continental countries alone refrains from taxing the imported watches and clocks, and is content with a merely nominal duty.

It may be that a country does not import in any quantity those commodities it chiefly manufactures; and that therefore the duty is useless; but the fact none the less remains that in each instance these manufactures flourish most when 'unprotected.'

On the whole, then, so far as Foreign competition is actually affecting British manufactures, we find that gradually the latter are obtaining easier access to the chief foreign markets. Any nation that still clings to the idea of a high tariff clings to an idea that has a pauperising effect : and in so far its powers are curtailed for purchasing English manufactures; in so far, its powers are curtailed of successfully competing in manufacture with those nations that enjoy all the industrial advantages of free intercourse with the rest of the world.

CHAPTER X.

§ 1. ONE of the commonest assertions on which is
founded an appeal to the State to do something for
English manufactures is that the *English home
market is being flooded by foreign manufactures.* We
must therefore form some idea of what this home
market really is, and of the place taken in it by
imported manufactures.

The British Association for the Advancement of
Science recently appointed a Committee to inquire
into the manner in which incomes were spent in
England.   Abundant statistics of all kinds were
collected and collated.   From the elaborate calculations of the Report of this Committee, it appears that

we probably spend each year in England on various manufactured commodities a sum approaching to 500,000,000*l.* Of these commodities we obtain only one seventeenth, or 30,000,000*l.* worth, from abroad.

This amount of foreign goods is roughly distributed as follows, and I add for comparison the values of our export of similar articles :—

	Imports.		Exports.
Silks and Gloves	£15,000,000	...	£3,000,000
Cottons and Woollens...............	10,000,000	...	80,000,000
Iron, Steel, and Glass...............	4,000,000	...	34,000,000
Miscellaneous	1,000,000	...	100,000,000
Total of these Manufactures	£30,000,000	...	£217,000,000

The silks and gloves are distinctly luxuries, and could only be purchased by well-to-do people. A large portion of the 'woollens' is to be credited to the influence of fashion. The chief feature, however, is the utter insignificance of the total sums as compared with the values of what we export. We probably send abroad ten times the value of the manufactured commodities we import.

There is, however, a fact of much importance in connection with this home market which largely regulates our dealings with foreigners. And this fact is the curious effect of fashion in the matter of clothing. Things have altogether changed in

this respect within the last fifty years Wear was
then the great attribute of good clothing; but now it
is so no longer.   There may be compensation in all
this.   It may be that a working man spends no
more on dress in buying a 1*l.* suit each year than
in paying 10*l.* for a suit that lasted him ten years;
or that his wife should buy a new 1*l.* costume each
year instead of a new 10*l.* gown every ten years.
But all this has a great effect on manufacture.
Districts and classes were formerly most conserva-
tive in the matter of dress, but now fashions
penetrate all over the country and through all
classes.   There is much more frequent change.
And where in old days this change of fashion
affected 1,000 people it now affects 100,000.

The sewing-machine — 'the printing-press' of
fashion in dress—has been the great and indispensable ally of this revolution.

A notable example of this effect of fashion has
been felt in the woollen trade.   The English woollen
manufacturers were slow to recognise this new
invasion of fashion.   The point was well if familiarly
put in the remark that women at one time made
balloons of themselves, and at another time mops.
At one time they were all for stiff, spreading, stand-
ing-out skirts, and at another all for limp, clinging,

close-fitting skirts. And as fashion had come to rule, not only in Hyde Park, but in every country town and village, this change in the material used for dresses had a most powerful effect on the trade. In this case in particular English manufacturers were slow to believe that fashion had so great an influence on the trade. But now that the lesson has been learnt, a more watchful eye will follow or anticipate the vagaries of fashion.

A change of fashion has all this widespread effect; but it must be mistaken neither for our industries being defeated in competition with those of foreign nations, nor for effects of depression among consumers. Fashion is a factor in our industrial and commercial life that has put on a new power lately, and one we must seek to understand and to acknowledge. And it has nowhere so great an effect as in the English home market. What with lowering of prices and raising of wages the great bulk of the people in England have now more to spend on dress and the accessories of life than any people have ever had elsewhere or in any other age. This fact not only widens the domain of fashion, but also gives to the English home market an importance in the national economy that makes it paramount to all other elements.

§ 2. If it be true that the English home market is now being flooded with foreign manufactures to the detriment of home manufactures, we shall find necessarily that the percentage of manufactured articles to the rest of our imports is increasing. It is thus well worth tabulating the actual facts of the case.

TABLE.

PERCENTAGE OF MANUFACTURED ARTICLES TO THE TOTAL OF IMPORTS AND EXPORTS OF THE UNITED KINGDOM FOR THE LAST FIFTEEN YEARS.

	IMPORTS.			EXPORTS.		
YEAR.	Manufactures.	Total.	Percentage of Manufactures to Total.	Manufactures.	Total.	Percentage of Manufactures to Total.
	£	£		£	£	
1867	17,600,000	27,200,000	7	175,700,000	181,000,000	97
1868	19,900,000	294,700,000	7	174,300,000	180,000,000	96¼
1869	20,700,000	295,500,000	7	188,800,000	190,000,000	96¾
1870	27,200,000	303,300,000	9	194,100,000	200,000,000	97½
1871	20,500,000	331,000,000	6	217,403,000	223,000,000	97½
1872	22,200,000	354,700,000	6	249,300,000	256,000,000	97¾
1873	23,500,000	371,300,000	6	247,800,000	255,000,000	97¼
1874	25,600,000	370,100,000	7	233,000,000	240,000,000	97
1875	27,100,000	373,900,000	7	215,300,000	223,000,000	96¼
1876	27,700,000	375,200,000	7	194,700,000	201,000,000	96 ⁶⁄₁₀
1877	28,800,000	394,400,000	8	192,700,000	199,000,000	96¼
1878	29,600,000	368,800,000	8	186,900,000	193,000,000	96¼
1879	29,000,000	363,000,000	8	186,000,000	122,090,000	96⅝
1880	33,200,000	411,200,000	8	215,000,000	223,000,000	96¹⁰⁄₁₂

From this table it is seen, once and for all, that for the past fifteen years our foreign trade in manufactured commodities has maintained a steady relative level; and that there has been no appreciable decrease in our relative exports nor increase in our relative imports of manufactured to other commodities. As our population increases in numbers and in wealth, it would be a very suspicious sign indeed if we did not spend some of our increased gains in the purchase of greater values of foreign manufactured commodities. But that at the same time we increase in equal ratio our purchases of raw material and of food is clear irrefragable evidence that our manufacturing ability is not in the least impaired. In short, these records distinctly show that to say that our home market is being flooded by foreign manufactures is to reverse the truth. As a matter of fact we continue to flood foreign markets, and we continue to spend more and more in our home market, but the proportion of foreign manufactures to native purchased in that home market does not increase in like ratio.

§ 3. It will not be altogether unprofitable to investigate one or two particular instances as to our foreign trade in certain specific manufactures. The most frequent public complaints have been in regard to hardware, silk, and woollens.

We are frequently informed that American cutlery and tools are driving those of English manufacture

out of the shop windows. We are frequently informed that continental, and especially American,
competition is altogether upsetting our hardware
trade. The following tabulated record of what is
actually happening will assist us to a correct
judgment :—

TABLE.

IMPORTS AND EXPORTS OF HARDWARE AND MANUFACTURED
METALS BETWEEN THE UNITED KINGDOM AND THE FOUR
COUNTRIES WE PRINCIPALLY DEAL WITH.

	1880.	
	Exports to	Imports from
France	£1,240,000	£228,000
Belgium	569,000	860,000
Germany	1,667,000	190,000
United States	5,075,000	281,000
Total	£8,551,000	£1,559,000
Other Countries	16,597,000	1,745,000
Total to all	£25,148,000	£3,304,000

If French and German and American cutlery and
tools and machines are flooding the English market,
what shall be said of English goods of the same
kind in those markets ?—at all events we are
returning the compliment fiftyfold.

And if we look into the silk trade we find similar
evidence; and yet we not unfrequently hear that
the silk trade at all events has been ruined. Even
Free Trade orators have comforted the Coventry

mill-hands by pointing out that though the one industry of silk manufacture has slipped from their grasp, its place has been occupied by the manufacture of bicycles. The following details as to our annual exports of 'silk manufactures' may be interesting:—

	1869.		1880.
France . . . ·	£114,000	steady rise to	£577,000
Germany	77,000	,, ,, ,,	110,000
United States	279,000	uneven fall ,,	218,000
Belgium	Nil.	steady rise ,,	56,000
Canada	22,000	,, ,, ,,	84,000
India	10,000	,, ,, ,,	355,000
Australia	66,000	,, ,, ,,	205,000
Other Countries	542,000	uneven fall ,,	425,000
	£1,110,000	steady rise to	£2,030,000

	1869.		1880.	
Exports of Silk } Manufactures }	£1,110,000	rise to	£2,030,000	increase 90 per cent.
Imports of Silk } Manufactures }	11,800,000	,,	13,100,000	,, 11 ,,

The tendency here again is to turn the tables on foreigners so far as flooding markets is concerned.

Another instance is that of the woollen trade. The facts of the case I condensed in a letter to the *Times*, which I will here reprint, as it contains evidence very much to the point:—

"At this meeting at the Mansion-house it was explicitly stated by the speakers, with the tacit acquiescence of the audience, that the English woollen trade was being overwhelmed by foreign competition, and that that mysterious despot Fashion marshalled and directed this new invasion. The leaders of the movement that is to oppose this conjectural invasion seem content to depend on mere allegations, and to be presumably not aware of the figures of their own trade. They may, therefore, be interested to know that transactions were as follows in the year 1880 :—Of woollen manufactures, in round numbers of value, we made and consumed in England 63,000,000*l.* ; we made and exported from England 17,000,000*l.* ; and we imported and consumed from abroad 7,000,000*l*

In other words, Fashion, marshalling to her support all the varieties and excellencies of foreign endeavour and skill, manages to supply us with one-tenth only of what we annually consume in woollen manufactures ; and, on the other hand, we supply foreigners with nearly three times the value of woollen manufactures that we obtain from them. The foreigner must be mightily unfashionable ; and it seems that his eagerness to possess himself of goods that are pronounced at the Mansion-house to be unfashionable enables the ladies of England, out of the profits of the trade, to wear whatever they may consider most suitable to their position, their person, or their purse.

It may also be interesting to the leaders of this new movement to know that we are year by year using more and more 'raw' wool in England. The following figures testify to this :—

	1870. Lb.	1875. Lb	1880. Lb.
1. Of Foreign Wools we Imported..	263,300,000 ...	365,100,000 ...	463,500,000
2. Of Foreign Wools we Exported..	92,500,000 ...	171,100,000 ...	237,400,000
3. Of Foreign Wools we retained for use ... ...}	170,800,000 ...	193,000,000 ...	226,100,000

It is also to be remembered that as a nation we are taking from foreigners more and more yarn for weaving and other manufacturing purposes. The figures are :—

	1870. Lb.	1875. Lb.	1880. Lb.
Yarns Exported	35,500,000 ...	31,700,000 ...	26,500,000
Yarns Imported	10,300,000 ...	12,400,000 ...	14,900,000
Excess of Exports	25,200,000 ...	19,300,000 ...	11,600,000

In other words, so far as the foreign trade in yarns is concerned, we are supplying less and less to foreigners, and taking more and more from them; and, as yarns are only used for manufacture, these facts do not exactly prove that foreigners are manufacturing more and we manufacturing less.

I would allude briefly to the other point—the alleged effects on British agriculture. Here, again, it is often better to know what is actually proceeding than to ignore such knowledge, and allow the kindly impulses of generosity to be led astray by the imagination. It seems to have been tacitly assumed that both prices and quantity of English-grown wool have fallen solely because fashion has for the time being deserted lustre and long wool for dulness and short wool. But the magnitude of this asserted influence is limited by the fact that of the 150 million lbs. of wool annually grown in these islands, 55 millions at the least are short wool. And, again, those familiar with agriculture know very well that for years past farmers have bred for the carcase and not for the fleece; they have found it more profitable ever since the beginning of the century to supply the butcher rather than the manufacturer; and the consequent fall in the value of the fleece has been more than compensated by the increased bulk and general character of the carcase; and meat is one of the few commodities that seem always to remain high in price. The number of sheep in England varies but little taking one year with another. The averages for the last four triennial periods have been—$32\frac{1}{2}$, $33\frac{1}{2}$, $32\frac{1}{2}$, and $31\frac{1}{2}$ millions. The figures always fall off in wet years. Fluke and other diseases incidental to excessive moisture are known to have almost decimated flocks in certain districts of late. The fashion for these dull wools, on the showing of the authors of this new movement, did not enter upon the scene till 1874. But in 1868 there were 35 millions of sheep in these islands, and in 1871 only 31 millions, in spite of the absence of all interference on the part of fashion. It is also worth while noting that the increase has been continuous in the export of English-grown wool, from 9,000,000 lbs. in 1870 to 11,000,000 lbs. in 1875 and 17,000,000 lbs. in 1880. Foreigners are taking more and more of our home-grown wool. The results on fashion may be disastrous, but we have no cause to complain.

When we meet with an appeal to English ladies to employ English labour in preference to foreign, we find ourselves face to face with an appeal altogether out of tune with the intelligence and tendency of the times. If education has achieved anything, English women will know they cannot spend a penny on French or any other fashions unless the penny has been earned first; English labour provides the English nation with the where-withal for these foreign purchases.

On this question of fashion the ladies of England will do well to follow the 'statesmanlike' lead of her Royal Highness the Princess of Wales, and not be led astray to imagine that by purchasing what they do not want they can in any way assist those whose economic function it is to supply what is wanted. British industries, as a rule, are quite capable of taking care of themselves; they require no patronising, and least of all would they brook any grandmotherly protection from foreign competition. *England manufactures nearly one-third of the wool that is manufactured in all Europe.* The English system is doubtless capable of improvement, but it is not trembling in its shoes because the general prosperity enables the nation to make a few purchases abroad. As long as we in England wisely and determinedly allow as little as possible to interfere with the free course of industrial transactions, fashion can but assist in giving spice and stimulus to industrial exertions.

To attempt to fight natural tendencies is a beating of the air that is vain, if it be not indeed actively injurious to the interests involved. And it is a fight which the wise will wage only when they are ignorant. A generous but purblind imagination has before now led good people to lay the lance in rest, even against innocent windmills."

By thus gathering together facts we see that even these three classes of manufacture, classes to which popular rumour has specially credited most ruinous effect from foreign competition, retains nevertheless all the outward signs of vitality, and of most successful competition against the dreaded foreigner. In short, there is not apparently any single instance of manufacture in England that is not doing at the least as well as those in foreign lands. And it is probable that the majority of these are prospering better, especially in regard to the export trade they can and do command.

It may be well to append to these particular instances an analysis of our exports to France during the last few years :—

TABLE OF EXPORTS TO FRANCE FROM THE UNITED KINGDOM.

	1869.	1874.	1880.
	£	£	£
Apparel and Hosiery......	99,000	116,000	162,000
Cotton Textiles	987,000	1,040,000	1,070,000
Silk	114,000	290,000	577,000
Woollen	551,000	1,128,000	1,441,000
Worsted	1,337,000	1,860,000	1,377,000
Earthenware	28,000	45,000	92,000
Other Manufactures	3,277,000	2,765,000	2,927,000
Total Manufactures ...	5,793,000	7,264,000	7,546,000
Coal...........................	879,000	1,876,000	1,552,000
Alkali	63,000	75,000	89,000
Metals Unwrought.........	941,000	857,000	905,000
Wool	380,000	242,000	63,000
Total Raw Materials ...	2,663,000	3,050,000	2,609,000

From these records it will be seen at once that so far as the French market is concerned we are increasing our hold upon it in regard to manufactures, but that we find the French require of us less and less of the raw materials which manufacturers make use of.

§ 4. If we look to England itself we shall learn much. The prosperity of the people, and more especially of those whose incomes are small, depends intimately on the purchasing power of money. A high tariff is always opposed to increasing this power. Its effect, if it has any, must be to raise local prices. Indeed a high tariff has no influence of a protective kind unless it raises prices above what they are in other countries. Even American authorities have to allow that the labourer in America, if this purchasing power of money be taken into consideration, is not so well off as the labourer in England. And the United States is only to a moderate degree affected by its high tariff, because all over its vast interior it upholds Free Trade. In the United States, for instance, the growth of corn and wheat and meat is practically unlimited; in England we can only grow half of that we consume, and yet in England the prices of food are not higher than the prices of the same in the United States. This is all proof of the maxim—"If cheap food is not brought

to the people the people will go to cheap food."
We have had in England a series of seven very lean
years, and yet prices of wheat and agricultural produce have not risen. The farmer as a producer has
consequently suffered : there has been no compensating rise in price for shortness in quantity of wheat
he produces. But as consumer, not only of food,
but of manures, implements, clothing, labour, and
all else, he feels the benefit of no rise in prices. And
above all, he has enjoyed the reflex action of living
on in a community where dearth of harvests has not
ruined the general prosperity. There have been no
famine prices to check industrial prosperity.

And another remarkable feature is the great
advance in steadiness of prices : not only has wheat
not risen but meat has not fallen. We open our
markets to all the world, and we are rapidly discovering a steady uniform price for our own chief commodities. This is of special value to the farmer,
because he can tell surely what he is working for.
When he knows that prices will not alter very greatly
he can tell beforehand what it will pay him to produce ; and he will not devote a year's energies and
a year of his farm and all its belongings to the production of something which in the outside vagaries
of market prices he may find valueless when he has

produced it. This steadiness of price, consequent on worldwide supply, is a main element in the steady prosperity of agriculture.

It has been calculated that the wage-earning classes of England win a quarter of wheat now at an expenditure of exactly half the amount of labour they had to give for the same quantity thirty years ago. This represents a very great advance. It accounts for the fact of the shortened hours of labour we in England can institute and yet compete with all other nations successfully. Our labour is more profitable, and one chief reason of this is that we have no high tariff taxing the ordinary commodities of life and transferring money from the pockets of the labouring classes to the pockets of the capitalists. It is not remembered so often as it should be that a protective tariff raises a revenue over and above that which finds its way into the coffers of the State. The tariff raises prices. In many protective States every hardware article, every yard of cloth, or piece of clothing or furniture, costs more because of the tariff. Every labouring man has to pay this increase of price, and a great part of this increase finds its way into the pockets of the manufacturer and distributor. This does not occur in England, and as a consequence the wage-earner is better off.

But there is another point we have to see to. If labour is nominally cheaper in England than in other countries, is it really as good ? We may answer decidedly in the affirmative. We shall do so if we go into details; we shall do so if we only look to the fact that competition is free not only to goods but to men ; and the English artisans and mechanics not only completely hold their own against all foreign invasion in England, but are to be found in almost every manufacturing centre in the whole world. And in each of these they are found holding prominent positions. We are told on the one hand that we cannot compete with France, for instance, because our Factory Acts limit us to fifty-six hours, while manufacturers in France obtain seventy hours work a week from their 'hands.' The answer to this is that we do compete. And if we do compete at so much less expenditure of time, we find at once we must be doing our work far more economically. This must not blind us, however, to the danger that State Interference, as embodied in the Factory Act, might at any moment cause serious injury to English industry if it prevented a natural change in the hours of labour due to any new change in the comparative efficiency of our labour and of foreign labour that was working under freer conditions.

A great deal has been said of our sad lack of technical education. We are in a transitional state. We abolished that State Interference which was embodied in all the old apprenticeship and other close trade regulations and traditions, but we put forward no substitute. Indeed, the State forced on the nation an altogether different commodity on the plea that it was a fair substitute. Reading, writing, and arithmetic were made the substitutes for technical education. We do not yet understand the full effect of the great error that was made when the nation, in its proper determined enthusiasm to educate itself, was altogether led astray by rashly assuming that the three R's represented education. The farmer has all along protested; and now, at last, the manufacturer is protesting likewise. And we must hope shortly to see a reform in our education policy, which will, at last, begin with some adequate definition of the term education.

Farmers have long pointed out that children who are probably destined to become agricultural labourers are practically better educated by being taught the technicalities and practical operations of agriculture than by being hurried through courses of reading, writing, and arithmetic. Both branches of education are good, but if you substitute the one for the other you will oftentimes obtain an adult 'educated,' but ignorant of all knowledge that can serve him honestly for his life's work.

And so it is with manufacture. The dead level of the three R's is to be imposed on all children alike at the sacrifice of all other training. This unforeseen tendency of the nation's first grasp on the great idea of a thoroughly national education policy will soon be checked, and we shall have some real and efficient substitute for those means of technical education—of acquiring training and knowledge in their real work of life—which close guilds and apprenticeship systems sought, however badly, to provide.

It is well for English labour that it can still com·pete with the world, even though it has been so hampered by a partial attempt at national education. It is one sure hope of the future that in this direc-tion—at all events, in the direction of technical education, considerable improvement is yet possible and probable.

§ 5. On the whole we see that foreign competition in manufactures is at the present a non-existent element in our position. We open our doors to the foreign competitor in every sense of the term ; and by our national prosperity, we, so to speak, invite him to do his worst. In spite of all this, the amount of manufactures he supplies to us is altogether insignificant if compared either with the amount of manufactures we supply to him or with the amount we supply to ourselves.

We remain, after what has been called 'forty years of disastrous one-sided Free Trade,' the one great exporting country of manufactures. We also note, that of the other countries, those export the greatest percentage of manufactures that have the lowest tariffs; and we are driven, if we look to experience, to adopt the maxim that "the export of manufactures proceeds in inverse ratio to the height of the customs tariff." This is not a theoretic idea, but merely a plain matter-of-fact account of what has actually occurred among nations. One-sided Free Trade has, at all events, enabled us as a nation to pay the lowest prices for everything we use or consume. The consequence is that, flourishing thus as consumers, we can, as producers, in the long run undersell all foreigners who attempt to compete with us, and who do not enjoy similar advantages. It is for this reason we have been able to make so much of our coal and our iron and our climate.

What a country can best produce is not confined to what its soil or its climate yield, but to what the whole of the conditions of its existence yield.

Character, skill, perseverance, and even traditions in the people are often quite as important as latitude, or mineral resources, or rainfall. Forty years of free traffic with all the world, so far as we could make it free, have enabled us to develop many invaluable national qualities and attributes. In addition to this, on the one hand we have been checked from wasting our energies on the production of commodities more cheaply produced elsewhere ; and, on the other, we have been enabled to establish and to obtain a good start in various other industries for which we have equal, but not superior, natural facilities to other nations, but of which other nations have deprived themselves by a variety of artificial restrictions.

As a matter of fact, nature is more bountiful in regard to particular products in some districts of the earth's surface than in others. A high tariff prevents, and a low tariff allows, a nation to profit by this fact. And a government which would aid its citizens in industry or commerce by interfering with their natural advantages, and obstructing free intercourse, must, in the long run, injure and impede, not only the commercial, but the manufacturing prosperity and advance of the people.

S

CHAPTER XI.

INTERFERENCE WITH OTHER NATIONS.

§ 1. Four General Principles.   § 2. Lowering Tariffs.   § 3. Fighting
Bounties.   § 4. Commercial Treaties.

§ 1. The Government of any one country is not
infrequently urged, *proprio motu* or from without,
to extend the active influence of its own commercial
policy so far as to interfere with the private and
public policies of other nations. I wish in this
chapter first of all to summarise the principles that
should lie at the base of all international commercial
policy; and then to apply these general principles
to the particular modes in which such interference
may be embodied.

I will formulate four general principles, and then
pass on to apply those general principles to these
modes:—to tariffs, bounties, and treaties. I ven-
ture to think it is no exaggeration to say that the
problem we here deal with is one of the most vital

importance to our national future. We in England
have again arrived, as it were, at cross roads in our
commercial progress. We had done so before when
we took the right road in 1846, and again when
we took a wrong turning in 1860.

If we review generally the principles that ought
to regulate our dealings with other nations in regard to commercial policy, we see at once that we
have two concurrent duties to perform. There is
our duty to ourselves, and there is our duty to
foreign nations. It is not only just as wrong, but
it is just as foolish, to forego the one duty as to
forego the other. In regard to our duty to ourselves we light upon a first principle which I need
not dilate upon It is a principle more generally
accepted than any other. It is the promotion of
our own prosperity. In regard to our duty to other
nations, ideas are more mixed. In the first place,
there must be international as well as national
freedom. In short, the liberty of each nation is
only confined within the limits of like liberties
in other nations. Our liberty does not authorise us
to do anything that robs other nations of a similar
liberty, and we must resent any such attempt on
the part of a foreign nation. We must neither
interfere nor suffer interference with this liberty.

With this proviso in mind we come upon a second
general principle—the promotion of the prosperity
of other nations. It is often forgotten of what very
great importance to our individual prosperity is the
prosperity of other nations. Many of us know the
bad effect of a famine in India or China on English
trade. But there is more than this. In the late
heated discussion in newspapers and elsewhere on
the free trade question one point seems to me to
have been altogether overlooked. Stated broadly,
this point is that much of the falling off in particular cases in our export of manufactures, and certainly
a most serious drag on any increased consumption
of our manufactures in certain countries, is,—not that
they are supplying themselves; not that protection
has fostered and developed in their midst rival
manufactories to ours—but that they heavily tax
each native in his capacity as consumer, and so
discourage and weigh down his efforts as a producer; they pauperise the nation, and render it less
able to buy from other nations. This is a fact
strangely overlooked. I do not, of course, say that
it is the case everywhere, but it is the case in
certain countries whose natural and virgin resources
do not assist the population to resist and overcome
the pauperising effects of commercial restrictions.

A third general principle that should regulate international commercial policy is the removal of all restrictions or obstacles to the free current of commercial and industrial life. Freedom to industries is the mainspring of industrial prosperity. Of course this freedom is like international freedom, a mere relation. It means freedom to do all that does not interfere with the same freedom in others. The chief function of Government is to watch over this essential condition to the existence of freedom. That is the final cause of the State's existence. The State which busies itself with other matters is likely to busy itself to the detriment of its subjects. The main condition of commercial success also is that the will, whether of the individuals or of the State, be left as free and as untrammelled as possible. The contravention of this principle leads to endless conflicts of interests and to strange breaches of justice. To say that commmercial intercourse must be as unrestricted by State interference as possible ought to appear to many to be a needless truism, and yet it is a principle more commonly violated than any other. Indeed, the true value of commercial intercourse is not commonly appreciated. Many have forgotten how Mill proved commerce to be 'a mode of cheapening production.' Commerce

is certainly a means to that end. The more we
import and export the cheaper we can produce.
Interchange of commodities implies saving in the
cost of production. It is this saving of price in all
the nation consumes that makes commerce a source
of national wealth. Each commodity imported represents normally so much labour saved in its
production. The more the nation imports the more
it saves in the cost of production. Unrestricted
commerce will regulate itself according to the actual
profits accruing to the community. Anything that
interferes with commerce is simply a curtailment of
these profits. There is an important corollary to
this principle which most people overlook. It is true
we must never seek to compete against greater
natural superiorities in other nations. But, at the
same time, we must never forget to compete against
equal or lesser natural superiorities. It is by not
attending to this latter wholesome rule that we have
allowed the silk industries of France to steal a march
upon us in the matter of better technical education
and a higher standard of taste. This rule specially
affects Ireland. There are many industries in which
other countries have no natural superiority to Ireland; and some industries in which Ireland and Irish
people have actual natural superiority. Yet these

industries do not now flourish in Ireland. Lately, however, an altogether wholesome private movement is on foot which will, we all hope, be pre-eminently successful in reviving in Ireland those industries for which Ireland and the Irish have natural facilities greater than, or at all events equal to, those possessed by other nations.

These three foregoing principles apply to our commercial policy in so far as it affects our industrial and national prosperity. But our commercial policy is also largely controlled by the need of enabling the State to perform its duties. In most civilized countries the commercial policy adopted has close connection with the question of raising State Revenue. This we are compelled to recognise in regulating our commercial policy. And the best general principle to act upon is to see that the collection of Revenue does not hamper commercial and industrial life.

§ 2. If we apply these four principles to tariffs, we must come to these conclusions. We have our own tariff and we have the tariffs of other nations. Low tariffs are everywhere desirable if we would realize our four principles of prosperity. A low tariff, by interfering as little as possible with the ordinary free current of commerce, does not in practice restrict

or direct production or exchange. There is consequently no waste of labour or of capital on the
production of commodities that can be produced
cheaper elsewhere, or on the importation of commodities that can be produced cheaper in the country
itself. A low tariff incidentally promotes commerce,
and so increases the profit or saving of labour
accruing from all exchange. It thus promotes the
prosperity of all nations. And besides this, so far
as the object of raising revenue is concerned, a
low tariff is right, a high tariff wrong—that is, if
we judge by results. A low tariff may practically
not interfere with the free current of commercial life
if we see to it carefully that it neither oppresses
nor relieves of oppression home as compared with
foreign or foreign as compared with home products.
For instance, we not unfrequently meet with the
argument that some home industry should be
relieved of taxation. This contention has reason
in it only if a like industry in a country trading
with us in that particular commodity is free of
similar burdens. But we are apt to forget that
foreigners pay rates and taxes as well as ourselves.
It is not so generally acknowledged as it should be
that a low tariff in the course of years yields
more actual revenue than a high tariff. We have

our two colonies in Australia—Victoria and New
South Wales. They are very similarly circumstanced. Victoria for the past ten years has had
a high tariff, and New South Wales a low tariff.
In Victoria the income from customs duties during
these ten years has remained about the same per
annum : in New South Wales it has steadily
increased. Another example is that of the United
States as compared with the United Kingdom.
During the past twelve years the English customs
revenue has maintained a steady level of 20,000,000*l.*
per annum, though the tariff has been low, and
even reduced during the decade. During the past
ten years, with a high tariff, the United States
customs revenue has fallen from 37,000,000*l.* in
1869 to 27,000,000*l.* in 1880. And we must remember that during this decade the population of the
United States has increased by 10,000,000 while
our own has increased only by 4,000,000. If we
add this direct result to the indirect result of
largely increased imports, each item of which brings
profit to the nation, we shall see that a low tariff
brings a vast balance of material benefits which
would overwhelm even the most extravagant pre-
tensions in the way of industrial benefit set up
by the advocates of a protectionist tariff. If we only

remember that we profit by imports even more
than we do by exports, we shall not go wrong.
We must keep our own tariff low; that promotes
our own prosperity; but is it also our desire to
promote the prosperity of other countries? For
both reasons, then, we wish other nations to have
low tariffs. How are we to accomplish this?

We are told to put on an equivalent tariff so long
as they maintain theirs. But such a retaliatory
tariff is an act of war. There must be economic
loss. Such a tariff can only be justified by success.
Where have we experience or reasons to prove that
such a tariff ever reduced any other tariff? The
cost of such an act of war would forestal much of
any ensuing profits. Such an act would breed many
evil indirect influences, which last for a long time
and which, in the everchanging arena of 'practical
politics,' may well outlast any succeeding period of
low tariffs, even assuming such a period ever came.
It is instructive also to regard the practical possibili-
ties of retaliatory duties in England to-day. In the
first place, were we to impose them, the opinion
must gain ground among other nations that we
have abandoned low tariffs. All might not think
so; but some would; and in so far the imposition
of retaliatory duties to force some nations to low

tariffs would increase the tendency of other nations to retain high tariffs. In the second place, we must either impose them for a term of years or until their object be accomplished. A term of years will be taken, especially by the more obstinate opponents, to be merely a term of waiting. No term of years puts us to the risk of pursuing a hurtful policy for ever, or, at all events, for long. We should bind ourselves, in self-contradiction, to that very policy which we were seeking to overthrow. In the third place, more than 90 per cent. of what we import is food and raw material, and to put duties on these is simply to commit industrial suicide. In the present political state of the world, the remedy for high tariffs is to keep our own low and free from all foreign interference. This is the surest means eventually to outlive the action of high or hostile tariffs. We must hold up to the world the example of successful fact. This is a remedy which has not yet been tried. In the case of England, we began it in 1846; but we left off in 1860, when we made the French Treaty.

§ 3. In determining on the principles that should regulate our conduct towards countries that give Bounties, we must above all keep our attention fixed on actual experience. Mr. Gladstone has said, in

regard to the notorious Sugar Bounties,—" We do
not regard with any satisfaction the system under
which an artificial advantage is given in our
markets to the products of foreign labour." But
this idea is applicable only in the event of their
products being sold in our market at less than their
cost of production. This would deprive our own
industry of legitimate employment; but only when
and if it takes place. The question remains, What
Bounties do actually give an artificial advantage
in our market to the products of foreign labour?
A great many people will name at once the Sugar
Bounties. Well, firstly, let us look to facts. In
regard to the countries that give these Bounties, it
is, of course, evident that the artificial advantage
comes from the pockets of the people at large.
Consequently all profits of this artificial advantage
is merely returning to a few of the people what all
the people have paid out. But there is the further
question, Are there any extra profits created by
these Sugar Bounties? If we turn to reasons we
shall light upon an explanation which no one seems
to notice. These bounties are drawbacks on export.
In other words, the ' bounty-fed produce' is
produce which has escaped contributing to the
revenue, and which yields in addition certain

surreptitious profits on the transaction. But to accomplish all these ends there must be a duty on sugar. The greater proportion, then, of all this labour is simply to overcome an obstacle to industry which we in England have most wisely abolished when we abolished the sugar duties. It is not known so generally as it should be that no State on the Continent gives Sugar Bounties. The bounty is obtained in spite of the Government, and by reason of the difficulty of assessing a duty and an equivalent drawback on raw and refined sugar. Each Continental Government knows this, and each wishes to abolish so faulty a system. The only method that can really succeed is the doing away with all duties on sugar; and seeing that sugar is so necessary a food, this would appear to be both wise and necessary, and English experience proves the entire success of the method.

But, then, there are other bounties not founded on drawbacks. The most recent instance is the institution of Shipping Bounties by France. Their object is to promote a carrying trade and a ship-building trade. And they are to accomplish this by turning to these trades labour and capital from other employments. Much must be lost to the community by such forced interference with industry.

Had France population to spare to earn a livelihood on the sea; had France more coal and iron in close proximity to harbours; were France a mass of good harbours standing midway between the Eastern and Western civilizations; had France committed herself to a low tariff for purposes of Revenue only; had France 10 millions of Frenchmen and 200 millions of native races under her own rule domiciled in all distant parts of the world;—France would have been the natural rival of England in all shipping affairs. But France has none of these things, and it so happens that England has them all. It is therefore not wise of France to endeavour to rival England in a special industry due to special environments which France does not enjoy. Moreover, we already see that Italy and Germany and Spain are talking of Shipping Bounties. To put on such a bounty is to invite—nay, rather to incite—other nations to do likewise, and thus, even if successful, it becomes more than ever a dead economic loss to the country, and the instrument of its own destruction.

It may be contended that while we in England are waiting for other countries to experience by sad disaster and loss the mistakes they have made, our own particular industries may suffer from temporary depression, and that thus, in order to promote our own prosperity and also that of the other nations, we should endeavour to put an end to all bounties. If we take the case of England and France we shall see the difficulty in our way. If we place countervailing bounties on our own industries we at once bring the two cases more on to an equality. But then that means that we reduce the natural advantage we now possess—a natural advantage which is only made the greater by the artificial arrangement adopted by France. Again, it is equally impracticable to place a duty in English ports on all shipping that receives bounties, because by so doing we at once put a premium on French ships visiting foreign and neutral ports. We have become the great carriers and builders by our natural opportunities, and in some measure by our rather unique low tariff. Nothing can eventually deprive us of this but similar conditions arising in some other nation. If France prefers to take millions a year out of the pockets of her people, to make what M. Tirard himself has recently called 'great and heavy sacrifices,' in order to turn labour and capital from more profitable to less profitable employment, and to waste the margin of labour and capital expended in this

production over and above what would be expended
were things left free, we shall indeed note the expense all this is to the French people. We shall
also note the fact that in so far as these bounties
succeed in diverting capital and labour from
other industries, in so far do they open up a
new gap for English industries to fill. We shall
note, too, that whatever success may attend this
new policy will have its first effect on those shipbuilding and carrying interests which exist by
sufferance under peculiar local conditions. The free
and healthy English industry will be the last to
feel their effects. We remember that the up-keep of
the ships of the French navy is nearly three times
as costly as that of English men-of-war. There
are not the same material facilities in France. All
this dead loss of a forced industry, coupled with the
direct burden of the bounty, renders it absolutely
certain that in the end England must win. And
this even without taking into account that for very
consistency's sake the logical French mind will yet
demand similar bounties for all other industries.

To destroy the Bounty System we must trust to
indirect influences. And among these the most
powerful is the care that the natural advantages
any particular industry threatened enjoys in Eng-

land be not in any way hampered. As we have successfully braved the Sugar Bounties by taking away all duty on sugar, so we can successfully brave the Shipping Bounties by removing all restrictions on the increase of our commerce, and promoting the efficiency and speed and comfort of our mercantile marine. The French bounties, in so far as they are efficacious, will greatly stimulate private skill and enterprise in England. England has still the great sources of supply of coal and iron, and she has that colder climate that is so essential to metal working. England must look to facts and let fancies alone ; put her trust in experience, and keep her tariff low. Then the force of nature will overcome all those artificial restrictions placed by other nations on their own industries.

§ 4. There remains the last of our particular inquiries—What principles ought to regulate our dealings with other nations in respect to commercial treaties ? Commercial treaties are bargains or contracts based on a state of warfare. To have a treaty at all you must assume that the two countries are in a condition of antagonism. In so far, then, as commercial treaties are treaties of amity, in so far are they good. But in so far as they are treaties of commerce, in so far are they

T

restrictions on commerce. Now, they may be restrictions on commerce itself being restricted, as
when Japan contracts not to levy more than three
per cent. on imported goods. We find that this is
the usual tendency of modern treaties; they are
bargains by which one nation contracts with another for greater facilities of commerce. But by
their very nature they also bind a nation to confine these facilities to some one or two other
nations. They only do away with restrictions on
one stream of commerce by placing restrictions on
other streams. They thus compel a nation to adopt
a more costly mode of obtaining certain commodities than it would adopt were its action free and
unfettered. It would thus appear that no commercial treaty is correct which binds the contracting
parties to any differential duties or tariff. Commercial
treaties that open up trade with another country
without, at the same time, restricting trade with
other countries, may be beneficial. Such are the
treaties by which England secures commerce with
China and Japan. The French Treaty is not one of
these. The treaty of 1860 was a decided departure
from Free Trade principles; it restricted our freedom in commercial dealings with other nations. We
gained indeed by the low duties France placed on

our goods; we gained by the low duties we placed on French goods; but we lost in other respects. For instance, other nations, Spain and Portugal, at once raised their tariffs against us, and by this French Treaty we lost our liberty of managing our own financial and commercial affairs as we might deem best. Mr. Chamberlain has told us " If the treaty negotiations with France break down, the English Government would be perfectly justified in dealing with the wine and spirit duties as they thought best for the interests of the country." In other words the treaty, if made, will deprive the English Government of its liberty to deal with duties tending to the best interests of this country. We obtain, indeed, entry into the French market, but in so doing, if we may judge by experience, we close other markets to ourselves. That is sufficient of itself to condemn the treaty. But the question remains—Is this treaty the only means of gaining entry into the French market ? Now, if we declare to all the world we will make no contracts that bind ourselves, but will, from time to time, put on and take off duties as suits our own financial policy, will not such a policy afford them strong reason to open their ports to us in order to maintain commercial intercourse ? We might well tax some luxuries more than we do, and our wine

duties might well be readjusted. In these matters
our hands have been hitherto tied by treaties. In the
present condition of the world England would find
much saving of labour could her commercial treaties
be restricted to one clause—that known as 'the most
favoured nation' clause. Thus we should contract to
grant to all nations the fullest favours our domestic
policy will allow; we should contract to receive
from these nations the fullest favours their domestic
policy will be able to grant. But we should leave it
to each nation to elaborate its own domestic policy.
If we abide by profitable principles of conduct we
shall not make commercial treaties that restrict our
financial policy, or that in any way, directly or
indirectly, restrict our trade with third countries.
It will be better for our prosperity to have no
treaties at all than treaties that in any way bind
us. We are more likely to lead other nations to
lower their tariffs by such action than by that
vain seeking after reciprocal concessions which has
been attempted now for more than sixty years, and
which, whenever it meets with success in one
country causes, *ipso facto*, an equivalent backsliding
in other countries. If we have a treaty at all it
would be well if it consisted of the one clause—'the
most favoured nation' clause. Even this is merely

a conditional arrangement — conditioned by the peculiar political relation of nations to one another at the present day. A treaty is the only means existing, with the exception of warfare, for preventing one nation from pressing its own liberty so far as to encroach upon a similar liberty in other nations.

In thus considering what principles ought to govern our dealings with other nations as respects tariffs, bounties, and commercial treaties, I tabulate four principles: — 1, We must promote our own prosperity; 2, We must promote the prosperity of other nations; 3, We must free from all restraints and obstacles the courses of commerce and industry; 4, We must not allow the collection of revenue to hamper commercial or industrial requirements.

These principles are largely conditioned by the political relations of nations, but in applying them to the special objects under discussion we shall see that they lead us in regard to tariffs simply to keep our own as low as possible; in regard to the bounties avoid them altogether; in regard to commercial treaties, to make none that in any detailed way hamper our own liberty of financial or commercial action. These solutions proceed on the sound and profitable principle of assuring, both to ourselves and to others, the utmost individual freedom compatible with the like individual freedom of each other. By such courses we shall, in doing our duty to ourselves, also do our duty to other nations. And if we win in the race it will be because other nations handicap their own chances by unnecessary and hurtful restrictions on the liberty of the individual.

FINIS.

INDEX.

INDEX.

LONDON : R. CLAY, SONS, AND TAYLOR, PRINTERS.

Printed in the United States
By Bookmasters